Aristophanes: *Peace*

Bloomsbury Ancient Comedy Companions

Series editors: C.W. Marshall & Niall W. Slater

The Bloomsbury Ancient Comedy Companions present accessible introductions to the surviving comedies from Greece and Rome. Each volume provides an overview of the play's themes and situates it in its historical and literary contexts, recognizing that each play was intended in the first instance for performance. Volumes will be helpful for students and scholars, providing an overview of previous scholarship and offering new interpretations of ancient comedy.

Aristophanes: Peace, Ian C. Storey
Plautus: Casina, David Christenson
Terence: Andria, Sander M. Goldberg

Aristophanes: *Peace*

Ian C. Storey

BLOOMSBURY ACADEMIC

LONDON • NEW YORK • OXFORD • NEW DELHI • SYDNEY

BLOOMSBURY ACADEMIC
Bloomsbury Publishing Plc
50 Bedford Square, London, WC1B 3DP, UK
1385 Broadway, New York, NY 10018, USA

BLOOMSBURY, BLOOMSBURY ACADEMIC and the Diana logo are
trademarks of Bloomsbury Publishing Plc

First published in Great Britain 2019

Cover design: Terry Woodley

Cover image: Peace (Eirene) with the infant Wealth (Ploutos).
Roman copy of a 4th-century original by Cephisodotos, Glyptothek, Munich.
Erin Babnik/Alamy Stock Photo

A catalogue record for this book is available from the British Library.

Library of Congress Cataloging-in-Publication Data
Names: Storey, Ian Christopher, 1946– author.
Title: Aristophanes: Peace / Ian C. Storey.
Description: London : Bloomsbury Academic, 2018. | Includes bibliographical
references and index.
Identifiers: LCCN 2018024990| ISBN 9781350020214 (pb) |
ISBN 9781350020238 (epub)
Subjects: LCSH: Aristophanes. Peace.
Classification: LCC PA3875.P23 S867 2018 | DDC 882/.01—dc23 LC record
available at https://lccn.loc.gov/2018024990

ISBN: HB: 978-1-3500-2022-1
        PB: 978-1-3500-2021-4
        ePDF: 978-1-3500-2024-5
        eBook: 978-1-3500-2023-8

Series: Bloomsbury Ancient Comedy Companions

Typeset by RefineCatch Limited, Bungay, Suffolk
Printed and bound in Great Britain

To find out more about our authors and books visit www.bloomsbury.com
and sign up for our newsletters.

For Robin & Holly,
Miles & Dexter

"For I take no pleasure in battles,
but in drinking down wine
with good friends,
kindling a fire from logs
that have dried well over the summer"
(Peace 1130–5)

and in memory of James Morwood (1943–2017)

Contents

Illustrations

Titles and Abbreviations

APGRD   Archive of Performances of Greek and Roman Drama (Oxford).

F   a fragment of a lost work from antiquity. For the dramatic poets the fragments of Aristophanes are conveniently collected at Henderson 2007, those of Aeschylus at Sommerstein 2008, those by Sophocles at Lloyd-Jones 1996, and those by Euripides at Collard and Cropp 2008a/2008b. The other comic fragments can be found at *PCG* (see below).

FGrHist   Jacoby, F. *Die Fragmente der griechischen Historiker.* Leiden: Brill. 1923–58.

IG i³   Lewis, D.M. and L. Jeffrey (eds). *Inscriptiones Atticae Euclidis anno anteriores* 3rd ed., 2 vols. Berlin. 1981, 1994.

Koster   Koster, W.J.W. *Scholia in Aristophanem, Pars 1 Fasc. IA, Prolegomena de Comoedia.* Groningen: Boema's Boekhuis. 1975.

PAA   Traill, J. (ed.). *Persons of Ancient Athens*, 22 vols. Toronto: Athenians. 1994–2016.

PCG   R. Kassel and C. Austin (eds). *Poetae Comici Graecae*, 8 vols. Berlin: de Gruyter. 1983–2001.

POxy.   The Oxyrhynchus Papyri.

PSI   Papiri della Società Italiana.

TrGF I   Snell, B., S. Radt and R. Kannicht (eds). *Tragicorum Graecorum Fragmenta*, vol. I, 2nd ed. Göttingen: Vandenhoeck and Ruprecht. 1986.

When referring to a comedy by Aristophanes I have used an English full-title, *Thesmophoriazusae* being rendered as *Women at the Festival* and *Ecclesiazusae* as *Women at the Assembly*. To cite a particular line or passage, I have used abbreviations for *Acharnians* (*Ach.*). *Knights* (*Kn.*), *Clouds* (*Cl.*), and *Lysistrata* (*Lysist.*).

Dates should be assumed to be BCE. The designation CE is appended for ancient dates in the Common Era, but not for medieval and modern dates.

Introduction

At the City Dionysia in 421, Aristophanes' *Peace* won the second prize in the competition for comic drama, but the comedy was sufficiently well regarded to be included among the eleven plays which later scholars established as the 'short list' for this comic poet. Aristophanes (career: 427–*c.* 385) is for us the primary exponent of what the ancients called 'Old Comedy', being the only poet from that period for whom we possess complete comedies. This raises questions for which we can provide only partial answers: why the plays of Aristophanes survived when those of other comic poets did not, was Aristophanes the best or the most successful of these poets, or more important perhaps, were his plays typical of what was being staged in the late fifth century at Athens?

Critics and producers tend to highlight three of Aristophanes' extant plays: *Clouds* (a partially revised version of an original performed at the City Dionysia of 423), *Frogs* (the winning comedy at the Lenaea festival of 405), and in the last half-century on *Lysistrata* (produced in 411). The first certainly owes its popularity to the extended caricature of Socrates in the comedy, the second to the dramatic contest in the Underworld between Euripides and Aeschylus, two of the three 'canonized' tragic poets, and the third to its twin themes of 'women in control' and 'make love, not war', which resonated strongly with Western society in the last third of the twentieth century. But there is much about *Peace* that rewards scholarly investigation, appeals to those who want to experience a drama from another culture, and challenges actors and producers in the modern theatre. Since 1915 over one hundred productions of *Peace* have been staged both in the original Greek and in translation. Some of these were highly professional efforts and enjoyed successful runs in more than one venue.

The play possesses two brilliant visual scenes: the aerial ride of the comic hero from his home in Athens to Zeus' palace on Mount Olympus and the tug-of-war that drags Peace out of the cave where she has been imprisoned. The first is not only a clever parody of Euripides' recent tragedy, *Bellerophon* where that tragic hero appeared mounted on Pegasus intending to fly to Olympus and confront the gods, but a wonderfully funny scene in its own right, as the mood and language shift from the tragic to the bathos of comedy. Instead of a noble stallion, the comic hero harnesses a gigantic dung-beetle for his flight. This gives rise to all sorts of jokes about a dung-beetle's diet, defecation and excrement, outhouses etc. But beneath the comic fun Aristophanes may be making a more serious contention that while tragedy may consider itself the more serious form of drama, it is in fact comedy, and in particular Aristophanes' comedy, that can provide solutions to Athens' problems. Aristophanes coined a term for his sort of comedy, *trygōidia*, which has a connection to the name of the main character in *Peace*, Trygaeus.

This comic 'hero' is probably the most straightforward and appealing of Aristophanes' leading characters, lacking the rough edges or the self-centredness or the exasperating behaviour of some of the others. He is a simple son of the countryside, an expert grower of grapes and figs, who wants nothing more than to return to his idyllic life in the country before the war. This is what his wild mission to heaven achieves, the rescue of the imprisoned goddess of Peace, her return to Athens and installation as a presiding deity, and at the end his marriage to a divine handmaiden, celebrated by the formal procession back to the country.

Above all this is a comedy full of the beauty of the Greek countryside and of an ideal rural life before the War, with the optimism that this can all be regained with the return of Peace. When Trygaeus announces the impending rescue of Peace, the chorus cannot stop dancing for joy, and for much of the play they sing and chant some lovely lyrics about the blessings that Peace brings in her wake: social harmony, abundant crops, delicious fragrances, lots of wine, an ease of life, and an end to the hardships of warfare. Trygaeus' song at the end sums up well what Aristophanes is doing in this comedy: 'let us pray to the gods to grant wealth to the Greeks, for all of us to grow abundant crops and also much wine, for our wives to bear children, and to restore all that we have lost, and for the gleaming sword of war to be gone' (1320–8). Another reason to read or watch *Peace* is that Thucydides in the fifth book of his histories (5.13–24) provides a contemporary and detailed account of the events that led up to the signing of the peace treaty just two weeks after the performance of Aristophanes' play. Thus we can read or watch the comedy aware of the historical background or read the histories with the benefit of knowing how this treaty was being received in a war-weary city.

I must acknowledge first the unfailing support from the series editors, Niall Slater and Toph Marshall, friends and valued colleagues for many years, with whom it was my great pleasure to work more formally on this companion. At my home university I have to thank especially Kim Stanley and the Interlibrary Loans office, who located and obtained all sorts of items for me, at a time when the Library was in temporary quarters during major renovations. George Kovacs, Jennifer Moore and Donald Sells were always available to provide assistance and field my questions about whatever matters surfaced along the way. Stelios Chronopoulos (Freiburg) very generously shared with me his work-in-progress on *Peace*, and Angie Varakis (Kent) was a valuable source about the Greek production of *Peace* by Karolos Koun in 1977. A young friend, Dexter Lathangue, gave me the benefit of his prodigious knowledge of the world wars of the last century, and the Archives for the Production of Greek and Roman Drama in Oxford could not have been more helpful and accommodating. I have had only the best of relations with the staff at Bloomsbury Publishing with whom it has been a delight to work.

Finally, and on a sad note, as the first draft reached its final stages, I learned of the sudden passing of my close friend and colleague, James Morwood (September 2017). I was looking forward to discussing this first draft on *Peace* with him at our favourite dining-place in Oxford. This volume is dedicated to his memory.

Old Comedy, Aristophanes and a Play About Peace

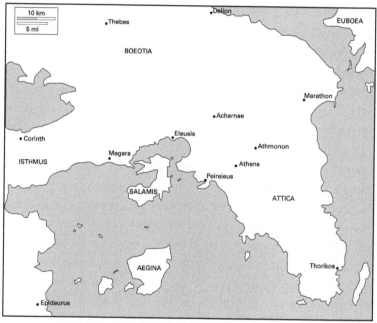

Figure 1.1 Map of Attica and surrounding regions.

Old Comedy

The ancient Greek word for comedy was *kōmōidia*. The philosopher Aristotle, writing in the fourth century BCE, says that 'because it was not taken seriously first, the origins of comedy have been forgotten' (*Poetics* 1449a36–b3), and then proceeds to fill that gap with assertions that may or may not be based on substantive evidence. He maintains

that for some comedy was a creation of the Dorian Greeks,[1] because
drama ('action') was allegedly a Dorian word and *kōmōidia* was
supposedly derived from *kōmē* ('village') and *ōdē* ('song'), *kōmē* being a
Dorian term for 'village'. It seems more likely, however, that the term
comes from *kōmos* and *ōdē* ('revel-song'), the *kōmos* being an exuberant
outdoor procession at public celebrations. According to Aristotle the
Dorian origin was also supported by the existence of something called
'Megarian Comedy', Megara being the name of two Dorian cities, one in
mainland Greece and the other in Sicily, and also by the known activity
of the comic poet Epicharmus, writing in Dorian Greek, at Syracuse in
Sicily in the early fifth century before the formal introduction of
comedy at Athens.[2]

Aristotle goes on to say (*Poetics* 1449b) that before comedy became
an official part of the Athenian dramatic competitions, any comic
performances were unstructured and performed by 'volunteers', and
that while tragedy developed 'from those who led the dithyramb', an
assertion for which there may be some justification, comedy came 'from
those who led the phallic songs which are still celebrated'. This may just
be Aristotle working backward from performances in his own time and
postulating these as the ancestor of comedy. If comedy did originate in
the *kōmos*, vase-paintings from the sixth century may perhaps be a
more reliable source that later literary commentary, as they reveal that
a *kōmos*, centred on the figure of the god Dionysus, was becoming a
popular feature of Athenian life by that time. Aristotle also uses the
adjective *iambikē* ('iambic') to describe early comic performances. This
term originally referred to a metrical scheme, but later applied to
personally abusive poetry which employed that metre:

> the creation of plots originally came from Sicily, and of Athenian poets
> Crates was the first to abandon the *iambikē* form and to create tales
> and plots on a larger scale.
>
> *Poetics* 1449b5–8

Ritual insults were part of the festive processions at the Athenian
Lenaea and Eleusinian Mysteries, at the former against the spectators

and at the participants in the latter case, and the personal humour that made Old Comedy distinctive may come from a combination of poetic tradition and festival insults. It is not clear whether Aristotle included the personally abusive comedy of Aristophanes and Eupolis in the 'iambikē form', or whether he means an earlier stage in Greek Comedy. Comic drama is known to have flourished in Sicily a little earlier than at Athens and this could have influenced the developing Old Comedy there, but a more likely influence is that of tragedy, established some years before comedy at Athens and certainly a narrative-based form of drama.

Whatever its exact origins, it is at Athens that comedy flourished most prominently in the fifth century. The canonical date for its introduction to the competitions at the City Dionysia there is 486, a date which most recent studies have accepted as not too far off the mark.[3] Comedy was the latest of the three dramatic genres to become part of the public festival. Tragedy was introduced in the late sixth century; the traditional date is 534, but a strong case can be made for a later date, in the decade 510–500. Then satyr-drama was added around 501. Comic productions continued to be produced at Athens and elsewhere in the ancient Greek world until well into the third or even second centuries. Ancient scholars, probably following the lead of Aristotle, whose first reaction to anything was to classify and sub-divide it, identified three phases for comedy, called 'Old' (usually *archaia*), 'Middle' (*mesē*) and 'New' (*nea*), although the first such distinction, that by Aristotle (*Ethics* 1128a22–5) records only two categories: 'Ancient' (*palaia*) and 'Modern' (*kainē*).

OLD COMEDY: *c.* 486 to the death of Aristophanes, *c.* 385
MIDDLE COMEDY: *c.* 385 to *c.* 325
NEW COMEDY: *c.* 325 to the mid-third century

Certain surviving anonymous treatises about ancient comedy have provided us with information of varying quality, some of it very useful

to the modern student. One such writer (Koster V) claims that Old
Comedy and New Comedy differed in several distinct aspects: time,
language, subject matter, metre and structure, but for the most part
these writers see the difference between Old and later comedy as
the political background and/or the presence or absence of personal
humour. For the latter, Aristotle) claims that for 'old' (*palaioi*) comic
poets *aischrologia* ('saying shameful things') was their source of
humour, while 'modern' (*kainoi*) poets employed innuendo. By
aischrologia I would understand both personal humour and what we
would call 'obscenity'. It is worth noting that Aristotle is writing before
the *début* of Menander (late 320s) and the beginning of what we call
'New Comedy'.

Platonius (Koster I, II), a writer of unknown date, attributes the
existence and success of Old Comedy to the freedom of the Athenian
democracy and the poets' ability to make fun of the rich and powerful.
Later comedy in his view was the result of the passage from democracy
to oligarchy, when 'fear fell upon the poets'. Ostensibly Platonius is
talking about Middle Comedy, but his reference to the oligarchs in
power ignores the fact that for most of the fourth century, the period
usually assigned to Middle Comedy, the government of Athens was still
a democracy. Platonius has confused the short-lived oligarchic regime
of 404 with the advent of Macedonian rule after 323 and thus ignored
sixty years of Athenian history. He continues and notice the emphasis
on personal humour (Koster I):

> the subjects of Old Comedy were the following: to censure generals
> and jurors who rendered bad verdicts, people who had acquired wealth
> through acts of injustice, and those who had adopted a sordid life-
> style. But Middle Comedy did away with such subjects and turned to
> making fun of poets for their writings, such as criticising Homer or the
> tragic poets for something they had written.

Middle Comedy may not be a substantive sub-genre as much as a
chronological one, i.e. between Aristophanes (died *c.* 385) and Menander
(début in the late 320s), a period without a single dominant poet.

Features often seen as typical of Middle Comedy, such as plays about the birth of gods and heroes, can in fact be found in earlier comedies of the 430s, such as Hermippus' *Birth of Athena* and Cratinus' *Nemesis* (birth of Helen). There is some debate whether Aristophanes' *Wealth* (388) should be classed as Old or Middle Comedy.

Even in the ancient world one hundred years is a long time for any art form, and we would not expect Old Comedy to have remained essentially static, but to have changed over that period. Investigating Old Comedy is complicated by the fact that we have extant plays for only one playwright, Aristophanes (career: 427–*c*. 385), eleven comedies spanning the years 425 to 388. While we do know quite a bit about certain other comic poets: Eupolis (career: 429–411), Cratinus (career: 454–423) and Pherecrates (career: *c*. 440–400), most of what we know covers the last third of the fifth century. For the first forty or so years we know little more than the name of Magnes, a remarkably successful playwright (see *Kn.* 520–5), and the transition into Middle Comedy is also shrouded in mystery.

The next chapter will examine how *Peace* fits into the larger genre called Old Comedy. It will be sufficient here to summarize the high points of this form of popular drama, remembering that not every comic poet wrote the same sort of comedy and that there were undoubtedly vogues during that century. 'Farce' is perhaps a better word than 'drama', since for the most part Aristophanes' surviving plays lack the solid linear plot that 'drama' suggests. Plays were focused around a 'great idea', an exuberant and imaginative fantasy, the more bizarre the better, and the humour depended on first realizing this great idea, such as Dicaeopolis defending his personal peace with the Spartans in *Acharnians*, and then watching the (il)logical developments that ensued. The chorus played a major role in Old Comedy, often adopting the identity of animals (*Birds*) or divine beings (*Clouds* or Phrynichus' *Muses*) or human groups such as cavalrymen (*Knights*), farmers as in *Peace* or initiates (*Frogs*). The chorus can be an active opponent of the idea (as in *Acharnians*), an enthusiastic supporter (as in *Peace*), or a more passive observer (as in *Frogs*). But their songs and dances were

integral to the performance of Old Comedy. The official command to a
poet to begin his play was 'bring on your chorus' (*Ach.* 11).

We find also sophisticated parodies of philosophical ideas, of the
poetry of Homer and the earlier poets, and especially of contemporary
tragic drama, Aristophanes' favoured target being the tragedies of
Euripides. One of Aristophanes' preferred descriptions of his comedy
and himself as a poet is *sophos* ('clever'). Yet Old Comedy is marked also
by coarse and aggressive language, physical slapstick and bowel humour,
lascivious innuendo and overt sexual behaviour. Some play titles and
the fragments of Crates and Pherecrates suggest a more domestic form
of comedy, with emphasis on the household and with female characters.
But for the most part Aristophanes' comedy is centred on the *polis*
('city') and a frequent theme is how 'to save the city'. This political nature
of Old Comedy attracted the attention of the ancient critics and
continues to dominate the scholarly discussions today. The great
question remains for scholars: how serious were Aristophanes and his
fellows about the political figures and issues that formed the subject of
many of the plays? To put it another way, were they writing comedy or
satire? Later critics fastened on the personal humour that was so
prevalent in the plays and fragments that we possess. *To onomasti
kōmōidein* ('to make fun of by name') became the quintessential feature
of Old Comedy, and ancient scholars eagerly invented laws allowing or
restricting such humour and sought for a redeeming social value that
allowed such licence in the first place.

Two potentially perilous assumptions confront the student of Old
Comedy. The first is that Aristophanes was typical of the genre as a
whole. Often we read that 'Old Comedy was marked by . . .', where what
is really meant is that 'Aristophanic comedy is marked by . . .'. We do
have enough remains of the other poets of Old Comedy to form some
conclusions about their sort of comedy: over 150 lines of Eupolis'
comedy *Demes* (including 120 lines on three papyrus pages), a papyrus
of Cratinus' *Wealth-Gods* which contains the entry of the chorus
and part of a subsequent scene, and a plot-summary of Cratinus'
Dionysalexander, a mythical burlesque in which Dionysus assumes the

role of Paris for that famous judgement of the goddesses.[4] Both of these comic poets display considerable and significant similarities with the Aristophanic comedies that we have, but they show also that Cratinus in particular was writing a different sort of comedy. Approximately one-third of the comedies in the Old period were burlesques of myth (such as Cratinus' *Dionysalexander* or *Nemesis*), but Aristophanes seems not to have employed this theme – he preferred to make fun of myths as they were portrayed in tragedy, particularly that of Euripides. Gods and heroes do appear in Aristophanes, such as Hermes in *Peace* and Dionysus in *Frogs*, but the background is always present-day Athens. We have no conclusive evidence that Aristophanes wrote a comedy set in the mythical past.

Likewise, themes of a Golden Age (back then or out there) are common in Old Comedy. Athenaeus (267e–270a) lists several examples of this theme in a number of comic poets, a frequent feature of which is that humanity will enjoy food and drink without the need to work the land or prepare a meal. Rivers of gourmet cuisine will flow through streets, fish will leap onto the grill and roast themselves (Crates' *Beasts*, F 16–17). Aristophanes' comedies do end with problems solved and in some cases a comfortable return to the good old days, but this all takes place in the here and now at Athens. Even in *Birds*, where the two Athenians flee from their city to the birds and establish Cloudcuckooland in the heavens, the new city looks suspiciously like an Athens purged of its undesirable features. *Peace* does hearken back to an idyllic life in the country before the war, with a real sense that life *was* better back then. While Trygaeus claims to be acting on behalf of all Greeks, it is really Athens that becomes the real beneficiary of his efforts. Finally, one of the joys of Peace for Trygaeus is that he and his fellow farmers will be able to work the land again and enjoy the fruits of their labour. Henderson (2015: 146) sums up well Aristophanes' comedy as it relates to the larger genre of Old Comedy: 'if we simply list the main types of comedy that were popular in competition at the turn of the fourth century, we can easily see that Aristophanes was hardly paradigmatic'. The intensely topical and political comedy that we readily associate with Old Comedy seems to have enjoyed a popularity from around 430 to 400, the same time period as the Peloponnesian War and critical political events at Athens.

Later antiquity tended to take Aristophanes' superiority for granted, calling him 'the wittiest poet', 'the grand old master', 'the most illustrious of comic poets', 'the charming one', 'the most pleasing one', 'the amazing Aristophanes', and a couplet is attributed to Plato (*Epigram* 14), 'the Graces, seeking a sanctuary that would never fall, / in their search they found the soul of Aristophanes'. There remains, however, the unsettling fact that while we are given victory totals for many of the Old Comic poets, we are never given any figures for Aristophanes. Did he, like the tragic poet Euripides, enjoy relatively few successes in his career, especially at the City Dionysia? Again, like Euripides, did his reputation as the principal exponent of his genre develop later, due perhaps to Plato's attribution of Socrates' poor public image to Aristophanes' *Clouds* (*Apology* 19c) and his inclusion of the comic poet among the guests in *Symposium*? Aristotle's selection of Homer, Sophocles and Aristophanes as the exponents of epic, tragedy and comedy respectively (*Poetics* 1448a19–27) may also have been influential here. Certainly, by the Alexandrian age a canonical triad had been established for Old Comedy: Aristophanes, Cratinus and Eupolis.

We may have listened too closely to Aristophanes' claims in his comedies to have been creating a superior form of comedy that surpassed the inferior trash that his rivals were passing off as comedy. A typical example comes from the *parabasis* of *Peace* (748–50), where the chorus claim:[5]

> having done away with such worthless trash and ignoble buffoonery,
> he created for us a great craft and topped off his structure with grand
> words and concepts and far from vulgar jokes.

A great game was being played involving comic poet, his rivals, the officials and the spectators, and we need to be careful of paying too much attention to the posture adopted by a comic poet or his rivals.

Aristophanes

Aristophanes is the only Old Comic poet whose works have survived, eleven comedies spanning the years 425 to 388, from a recorded total of forty titles, perhaps forty-four. In addition, nearly 1,000 fragments have survived as citations and allusions in other writers, a few also through papyrus discoveries. He was probably born in the early 440s and was thus a close contemporary of Alcibiades, the charismatic *enfant terrible* of Athenian politics and society in the late fifth century. Aristophanes belonged to the deme Cydathenaeon, located in the city of Athens itself. That might mean only that his grandfather resided there when Cleisthenes created the 139 demes in his political restructuring of Athens in the last years of the sixth century, but his comedies do show a man wholly familiar with the life and politics of the city. Like other well-off Athenians he may have owned property in the country, since the comedies (especially those of the 420s, including *Peace*) hum with the joy of life in the countryside, especially the countryside in time of peace.

Aristophanes' Career (extant plays in bold)				
L = Lenaea, D = Dionysia				
427-L	*Banqueters*	(second?)	414-L	*Amphiareus*
426-D	*Babylonians*	(first)	414-D	**Birds** (second)
425-L	**Acharnians**	(first)	411-L	**Lysistrata**
424-L	**Knights**	(first)	411-D	**Women at the Festival**
424-D	*Farmers?*		408	*Wealth¹*
423-L	*Merchant-Ships?*		405-L	**Frogs** (first)
423-D	*Clouds¹*	(third)	393–391	**Women at the Assembly**
422-L	**Wasps**	(second)	388	*Wealth²*
422-L	*Preview*	(first)	387 or after	*Aeolosicon*
421-D	**Peace**	(second)	after 387	*Cocalus*
c. 418	**Clouds²**	(partial revision)		

The actual success of *Banqueters* and *Babylonians* is not certain but likely, based on Aristophanes' statements in the *parabases* of *Acharnians* and *Clouds*. The *Clouds* that we possess is not the original version that finished third at the Dionysia in 423, but one that was partially revised *c.* 419/8 and probably never staged. When the chorus at *Wasps* 1037–47 describe Aristophanes' comic activities 'last year' (423), they are likely referring to two productions (1037–42, 1043–7), the second of which must be the original version of *Clouds*. Since the description at 1037–42 does not sound anything like the *Clouds* that we possess, it is probably referring to a production at the earlier festival of the Lenaea in 423. The third hypothesis to *Peace* lists *Merchant-Ships* as another anti-war comedy by Aristophanes in this period, while *Farmers* seems also to be an anti-war play from the 420s.[6] Current scholarship assigns *Farmers* to the Dionysia of 424 and *Merchant-Ships* as the comedy at the Lenaea of 423. The records for the Lenaea of 422 show that Aristophanes finished second with *Wasps* and that Philonides won with *Proagon* (*Preview*). But any time an ancient source cites a comedy called *Proagon*, that play is attributed to Aristophanes. When we consider that Philonides, a minor comic poet in his own right, also produced some of Aristophanes' comedies, it seems likely that Aristophanes in fact presented two plays on that occasion. The festivals for the productions for 411 are not given by the ancient sources, but *Lysistrata* is usually assigned to the Lenaea and *Women at the Festival* to the Dionysia. There seem to have been two comedies called *Wealth*, one (lost) dated to 408, the other (extant) to 388, but it is unlikely that there was any thematic connection between these plays. Finally, ancient sources record that *Frogs* was given the unusual honour of a second official performance, but at which festival is not certain. The Lenaea or Dionysia of 405, the Lenaea of 404 or the Dionysia of 403 have all been suggested, each with overtones to the contemporary political climate.[7]

Inscriptional evidence shows that between 435 and 427 no new poet won the first prize at the City Dionysia. Aristophanes was one of a group of poets who burst on the scene in the 420s and challenged the established playwrights (Cratinus, Pherecrates, Hermippus, Telecleides) with considerable success. Eupolis and Phrynichus made their débuts in 429, Aristophanes in 427 and Platon (not to be confused with the philosopher of the next century) in 424. Consider that over the seven years of comic productions between 427 and 421 and with two festivals a year Aristophanes would have had fourteen opportunities to compete. The above table lists nine fairly secure plays, not including *Proagon* which Philonides may have produced for him. One could not go to the theatre, it seems, in the 420s without seeing a comedy by Aristophanes. To put it another way, Aristophanes produced about one-quarter of his total output in the first seven years of a forty-year career. His third comedy and the first one that we possess, *Acharnians* (425-L), shows a mature comedian at the top of his form and not a novice whose skills are developing. His first three plays were produced through Callistratus and Philonides, the latter himself a comic poet, and in the *parabasis* of *Knights* (507–50) Aristophanes claims that he was diffident about taking on such a serious role as producing comedy. But his motivation was not just youthful inexperience, since he used these men during the prime of his career (Callistratus for *Birds* (414) and *Lysistrata* (411) and Philonides for *Frogs* (405)).

Comedies were produced as part of competitions, held first at the festival of the City Dionysia in late March or early April, and then from around 440 also at the Lenaea festival in late January. Both were public celebrations of the god Dionysus, and both lasted several days and enjoyed state sponsorship in that wealthy citizens were required to bear the costs of production of tragedies + satyr-drama, dithyrambs and comedies. Such sponsorship was called a *chorēgeia* and the sponsor a *chorēgos*. Artistic competitions were not unusual in ancient Greece, as both the Pythian games at Delphi and the Panathenaia at Athens awarded prizes in what we would call 'cultural events'. Thus, a poet's fellow playwrights were also rivals, and Aristophanes' plays, as well as several fragments from his competitors' work, might suggest that the prevailing atmosphere was one of antagonism – see the quotation above from *Peace*. But there are also suggestions that poets co-operated with each other, that allusions to the work of others may not be as derogatory as we have thought, and above all that the comedians adopted a comic *persona* for the benefit of the spectators. *Wasps* 1015–59 has been plausibly interpreted as indicating three stages in Aristophanes' early career, the first 'assisting other poets not openly but in secret' – one of these 'other poets' might have been Eupolis.[8] Aristophanes' comic *persona* was that of the brilliant and sophisticated comic poet, who rose above the inferior level of his rivals' comedy, took on great issues and personalities, always for the benefit of his city. That he has not been as successful as he ought is due not to inferior artistry, but to unappreciative spectators and poor judging.

The performance of *Peace* in 421

The manuscripts that have given us the ancient texts of Aristophanes also preserved short introductions to the plays, called 'hypotheses'. Some of these give information about the circumstances of production: usually the year and festival, often the result (first or second or third prize), and the names of the other competitors and the titles of their plays. Nine of Aristophanes' eleven extant comedies can be dated in that way, although for *Lysistrata* we are given only the year (411 BCE). The end of the third hypothesis to *Peace* gives the following information about the play, 'in the archonship of Alcaeus [422/1] Eupolis won first prize at the City [Dionysia] with his *Spongers*, Aristophanes was second with his *Peace*, Leucon third with *Phratry-Brothers*'. Aristophanes' initial burst of activity is usually taken as ending with *Peace* in 421. This may be just a convenient date that coincides with the end of the first phase of the Peloponnesian War, and also because we possess no complete comedy until *Birds* at the Dionysia of 414. We may with some confidence assign two or three plays to the years 420–415, but our first-hand knowledge is otherwise limited for that period.

Since his début in 427, Aristophanes had won at least two first-prizes at the Lenaea, three if Philonides' *Preview* is in fact by Aristophanes, and probably one victory at the Dionysia with *Babylonians* in 426. His third-place finish with the first *Clouds* (Dionysia of 423) ostensibly annoyed Aristophanes, witness his chorus' comments at *Wasps* 1043–50, 'you let him down last year when he tried to sow a crop of innovative ideas ... he swears by Dionysus that never has there been a better comic production', and also in the revised *parabasis* of the version of *Clouds* (518–62). But again, this may be part of a comic stance on the poet's part, and in both passages he makes much of the spectators' failure to appreciate good comedy when they saw it.

Complicating the problem is the uncertainty of whether three or five comedies were being produced at comic festivals in the 420s. Inscriptional evidence for the 430s makes it clear that five comedies were performed and ranked in order, and the hypothesis to *Wealth* (388) lists five comedies as well. But for seven other comedies, all between 425 and 405, the hypotheses list only three comedies. The usual explanation is that during the Peloponnesian War (427–421) comedies were cut from five to three and one staged each day following the tragic performances, thereby cutting one day from the festival. For Aristophanes this raises the question: did the first *Clouds* (423) finish third out of three (last), or third of five (only the bronze medal)?[9]

Assuming that only three comedies were produced at the festivals in the late 420s, we know the titles of four of the six comedies performed in 421. The scholia to *Clouds* 553 date Eupolis' *Maricas* to the 'third year after' the original *Clouds* at the Dionysia of 423.[10] Inclusive reckoning brings us to 421 and since Eupolis certainly produced his *Spongers* at the Dionysia of 421, this leaves the Lenaea of 421 for *Maricas*. This comedy was a significant one in the rivalry between Eupolis and Aristophanes. At the Lenaea of 424, Aristophanes produced his *Knights*, an entire comedy attacking Cleon, a leading Athenian political figure. In the revised *Clouds* (549–62) he complains that Eupolis 'was the first, he dragged his wretched *Maricas* on stage', attacking not the now deceased Cleon but Hyperbolus, Cleon's successor as leading demagogue (*Peace* 679–92). Aristophanes continues to complain about Eupolis 'turning our *Knights* inside out', using the image of comedy as a piece of clothing. We do not know who competed against *Maricas*, but it would be a nice touch if Aristophanes were one of them.

At the Dionysia of 421, the three comedies produced were Eupolis' *Spongers*, Aristophanes' *Peace* and Leucon's *Phratry-Brothers*. *Spongers* was a play about Callias, a prominent young Athenian who had recently come into a considerable inheritance. While *Maricas* was a political comedy aimed at Hyperbolus, who had succeeded Cleon as 'leader of the people', *Spongers* made fun of the personal life of Callias, who was famous for his profligate life-style and for entertaining both harlots and philosophers. This comedy probably influenced Plato in his *Protagoras* and Xenophon in *Symposium*, both set in the house of Callias. Leucon is a little-known comic poet who produced comedies in 422 and 421 and later won a Dionysia victory around 410. A phratry was an Athenian social institution, a mixture of an extended kin group and social club. Membership marked one's status as a citizen and jokes are made against those who allegedly lacked such membership. The few fragments and the title suggest a social comedy, perhaps like *Spongers*. Unlike the other early comedies, *Peace* does not contain any direct allusions to the rival poets, only a general condemnation of inferior playwrights and the superiority of Aristophanic comedy at lines 739–42, 'the only one who put an end to his rivals always poking fun at rags and declaring war on lice, the first to banish from the stage an always starving Heracles kneading bread, and to do away with those cheating slaves running away and getting a beating'.

Some have attributed *Peace*'s second-place finish to its loose structure and lack of a real conflict, seeing it as an extended and effusive celebration of the coming armistice rather than a formal drama. Another suggestion is that the use of a statue rather than a mute actor did not go over well or was badly staged. But without possessing the first-place comedy, Eupolis' *Spongers*, we cannot say for certain that the problem lay with *Peace*. We do know a good deal about Eupolis' play, and it may well be that the clever portrayal of Callias stole the show on that occasion, especially if Callias experienced a catastrophic reversal of his fortunes in the play (F 162, 167, 169) at the hands of his creditors and the predatory chorus of professional spongers (F 172). Judging the dramatic entries was a complicated system and still not fully understood. A judge was appointed from each of the ten tribes and would cast their votes for the winning comedy; to discourage bribery only five of these votes would be counted, and a result determined.[11] Thus it is possible that one play could win seven of the ten first-place votes, but if the five uncounted votes were all for that comedy, then a play with only three first-place votes could have won. There are stories in the later tradition about the audience's reaction to an unpopular verdict, usually involving *Clouds*, and we do know that following the final performance at the festival a meeting of the Athenian assembly was convened in the theatre to assess the conduct of the competitions.

Summary of the comedy

The comedy opens with a pair of slaves engaged on what is clearly a disgusting and malodorous task, kneading cakes out of excrement for a monstrous dung-beetle stabled inside the house. One slave explains to the spectators that their master, who introduces himself at line 190 as 'Trygaeus of Athmonon, skilled at growing vines,'[12] is angry at the gods over the war with Sparta for so many years. His great idea is to fly up to Olympus and confront Zeus about why the gods have allowed the Greeks to suffer the woes of war, for so long. To accomplish this, he proposes to ascend to Olympus, not as Bellerophon did on his winged horse Pegasus, but on a gigantic dung-beetle. As Trygaeus, mounted on the dung-beetle, hovers in the air above his house, neither the slave nor his daughters can dissuade him from this mission. The actual flight is a sustained comic parody of Euripides' earlier tragedy *Bellerophon*.

After landing at the doors of Olympus, Trygaeus encounters the god Hermes, from whom he learns that Zeus and the other gods have abandoned Olympus, leaving the Greeks to the mercies of War, who has locked Peace up in a cavern blocked by rocks. War with his henchman Riot appears with a giant mortar, preparing to pound all the Greek states into a savoury-mash. He requires only a pestle to do the grinding, but Riot reports that he cannot borrow one from the Athenians or the Spartans, since they have both lost theirs. These stand for Cleon and Brasidas, the two leaders killed at the battle of Amphipolis in late 422. Trygaeus summons a group of farmers (the chorus) to assist in the release of Peace and with the connivance of Hermes they succeed in dragging Peace, represented by a statue, out of her cave, where she is enthusiastically greeted by all. In a subsequent scene, Peace asks Trygaeus through Hermes what has happened in her absence. The questions and answers have to do with both two contemporary dramatists and two political leaders. Finally, Trygaeus is sent back to earth with Peace's handmaids, Opora ('Harvest') and Theoria ('Holiday'), the latter a gift for the Athenian Council, the former for himself as his wife.

During the *parabasis*, the chorus praise the skill and excellence of their comic poet, and then sing a pair of songs denigrating the inferior efforts of certain tragic poets. Trygaeus arrives home and after some by-play with his slave sends Harvest inside to be made ready for her marriage and then hands Holiday over to the Council in a scene laden with sexual innuendo. The statue of Peace is now installed formally as a presiding deity with a formal address by Trygaeus and a sacrifice is begun. This is interrupted by Hierocles, a self-important oracle-monger who is intent on crashing the party and enjoying some of the sacrificial meats. In a second *parabasis*, the chorus sing of the delights of the countryside in a time of peace. Trygaeus next welcomes those who sell agricultural implements and deals harshly with an arms-dealer whose wares he converts to more peaceable and mundane uses. He celebrates his marriage to Harvest with a marvellous feast, at which two boys appear to sing. The son of the general Lamachus sings martial verses from Homer, while the son of Cleonymus (who, it is alleged, abandoned his shield in battle) chants a famous poem from Archilochus, who threw his shield away and survived to laugh (and write) about it. The comedy concludes with a rousing wedding-song to Trygaeus and his divine bride and the marriage procession becomes the formal return to the countryside now that the war is over and Peace has returned.

Peace as an Old Comedy

The comic 'hero'

The main character of an Aristophanic comedy is usually a determined individual engaged on a bizarre and fantastic mission. We should avoid the word 'hero' since no ancient Greek word corresponds to our concept of the 'hero' of a story or a film. *Hērōs* meant a semi-divine being or a human of great achievements, while *protagōnistēs* denoted the lead actor, not the character he portrayed. In the eleven extant comedies, the leading character is usually an older male, although in *Lysistrata* and *Women at the Assembly* a woman conceives and executes the great idea. Whitman (1964) tried to group all these main characters under a similar label ('comic hero') and to imbue them with what he calls *ponēria* ('wickedness') – 'roguishness' might be more accurate. But these principal characters do not all fit easily into a single frame. Rosen (2014) provides a very useful analysis and development of Whitman's definition of the 'comic hero'.

They often bear significant names. In *Acharnians*, Dicaeopolis ('Just City') defends his decision to make his own private peace with Sparta against a hostile chorus of men from Acharnae. In *Clouds*, Strepsiades ('son of Twister') goes to Socrates to learn how to talk his way out of paying his debts, while in *Birds*, Peisetaerus ('persuasive companion') and his friend Euelpides ('son of good hope') flee Athens to join the birds in their freedom and end up founding the city of Cloudcuckooland in the sky. At the end Peisetaerus marries Basileia ('Princess') and becomes the new ruler of the birds and perhaps even of the gods. Lysistrata ('she who breaks up armies') arranges a sex-strike among the wives of Greece to bring the War to an end – 'make love, not war' – and

Praxagora ('she who acts in public') in *Women at the Assembly* dresses her women-friends up as men to attend the Athenian assembly and vote power to the women.

Not all the comedies depend on this determined sort of chief character. In *Wasps*, the roguish figure may be Philocleon ('Love-Cleon') the father, but it is his son Bdelycleon ('Loathe-Cleon') who conceives and executes the great idea, that father should cease to be a juror at public trials and judge cases in the comfort of home. Likewise, in *Women at the Festival* the clever Euripides convinces his relative (the rogue figure) to infiltrate the assembly of the women and defend him at that gathering. In some plays the great idea is conceived before the action begins, as in Aristophanes' *Acharnians, Clouds, Peace, Lysistrata, Women at the Festival, Frogs* and *Women at the Assembly*, but in *Knights, Wasps, Birds* and *Wealth* the idea emerges as the play unfolds. For other comic poets it is virtually certain that in Eupolis' *Demes* the main character was an old man named Pyronides ('son of the fiery one'), whose great idea it was to summon up four dead leaders of Athens and presumably put things right within the city, and F 293 of Eupolis' *Friends* shows a scheming old man who has hatched some sort of clever plan that involves joining the cavalry.

The main character in *Peace* is called 'Trygaeus', which is not a recorded name in *Persons of Ancient Athens* (hereafter '*PAA*') and should thus be considered as a 'speaking name'. The first part can be related to the verb *trygān* ('harvest fruit'), and in the comedy he reminds us of his skill at growing and cultivating grapes and figs. A recurring theme of the play is that peace will restore access to the fruits of the countryside (520–600, 999–1005, 1127–71) and to the joys of life there. One of Peace's two handmaids is called Opora ('Harvest') and her marriage to Trygaeus is predicted to be a fruitful one, 'producing a crop of little grapes' (706–8). To some degree Trygaeus does resemble Dicaeopolis, the central character in *Acharnians*. War has displaced both men from their rural demes into the crowded city ('lusting after peace, hating the town, longing for my deme' – *Ach.* 32–3), Dicaeopolis complains at one point that 'my vines have been cut down too' (512), and both have formulated an imaginative scheme to achieve peace. But Dicaeopolis is personally more aggressive and his great idea is motivated as much by his own selfish pleasure as by any altruistic feeling for his city. Certainly, there is none of the Panhellenic theme that we see in *Peace*. Trygaeus wants a return to the countryside, the restoration of the idyllic life before the onset of war, and a communal existence for all to enjoy, except those who prosper through war. The Greek word for peace/Peace is *eirēnē* and denotes a state of tranquillity and freedom from hardship and worry.

There may be more to his name. On four occasions in *Acharnians* (499–500, 628, 886) Aristophanes presents a new word for comedy, *trygōidia* (*tryx* + *ōdē* – 'song'). *Tryx* means 'new wine' or 'the lees of wine', hence 'new-wine-song.' One ancient source guessed at the etymology by suggesting that before masks, actors used to disguise their faces by smearing wine-lees on them, but the term is more likely a coinage by Aristophanes. At *Ach.* 499–500, Dicaeopolis delivers his great speech to the hostile chorus, in large part a parody of Euripides' tragedy *Telephus* (438). He begins by identifying himself with Aristophanes and mentioning his run-in with Cleon after *Babylonians* in 426, by stating firmly that '*trygōidia* too knows what is just' (500). Obviously *trygōidia* is meant to recall *tragōidia* ('tragedy') and to set comedy in opposition to serious drama, Aristophanes' point being that his comedy should be taken seriously, since his jokes benefit the city (see *Ach.* 647–51). Thus, in a genre centred on Dionysus, the god of wine, not only is *tryx* an appropriate element of the name Trygaeus, a character whose skill lies with cultivating grapes and figs, but also fitting for the principal character in a comedy (*trygōidia*). There is not, however, the same direct identification between Trygaeus and Aristophanes as there is with Dicaeopolis in *Acharnians* or with Bdelycleon in *Wasps* (651–2), although when Trygaeus rides his dung-beetle to Olympus in a parody of Euripides' *Bellerophon*, he is standing in for the comic poet who created him.

His great idea is to fly to Olympus and confront Zeus with the sufferings of the Greeks and to discover what he intends to do to them. His first words are in tragic mode (62–4), 'What is that you would do to our folk, O Zeus? Do you not realize that you will be draining the life

out of our cities?' The tragic language and metre will continue through
the prologue as Trygaeus re-enacts in comic style Bellerophon's flight
on Pegasus. Likewise, in *Acharnians*, Dicaeopolis opens the play with a
paratragic declamation and later exploits another Euripidean play,
Telephus, in his confrontation with the chorus. But Dicaeopolis' great
idea is to make a peace for himself with Sparta, and the action is firmly
fixed on earth with no involvement of the gods. The opening scene of
Peace also resembles that of *Knights* (424-L), where two slaves open the
play and explain the situation, although they have not yet conceived the
great idea – this comes at line 145 after an oracle has revealed how
Paphlagon (Cleon) can be overthrown. *Wasps* (422-L) likewise begins
with a pair of slaves who explain the plot directly to the spectators
(*Wasps* 54-135 cf. *Peace* 50–81), but in that comedy the son, not his
father, conceives the great idea which will not be outlined until
considerably later. Trygaeus, like Bellerophon, will never get to confront
Zeus with his complaints. The only speaking deity that he meets is
Hermes who confesses that the gods, impatient with the Greeks for
continuing their conflict, 'moved out yesterday' (197), and left them to
the tender mercies of War (Polemos). War has imprisoned Peace in a
cave and is planning to pound all the Greek cities into a savoury-mash.
This leads Trygaeus to alter his great idea, no longer to confront Zeus,
but to rescue Peace from her cave and restore her to Greece.

In almost all the extant comedies, Aristophanes' main characters
realize their great endeavour and enjoy the benefits of the new order
that they have created. This is especially true of Dicaeopolis in
Acharnians, who by making his own peace with the enemy can now
trade with the Thebans for the coveted eels from Lake Copais and
ignore the hardships caused by war. He ends the comedy by winning a
drinking contest and is carried off in the arms of flute-girls, while
Lamachus the general, wounded while on patrol by tripping over a
wine-stake, is stretchered off to the medicos. Only in the partially
revised *Clouds* is the great idea seen to have been a mistake and the
main character repent of his decision, while in *Wasps* the son has
succeeded too well in persuading his father to give up judging law-cases

and enjoy the good life. The old man attends his first symposium, gets terribly drunk, and behaves outrageously. Next morning the old juror will be back in his familiar courtroom setting, but this time as the defendant in a case of assault. Some have seen the last scenes of the later comedies, *Women at the Assembly* and *Wealth*, as deliberately ironic, in that Aristophanes allows a great idea to succeed with which he personally disagrees (women taking over the state, enabling the blind god Wealth to regain his sight), but it is more reasonable to view these plays as straight fantasies, which do not rise to the same comic heights as his earlier comedies. F 131 of Eupolis' *Demes* shows that the great idea, raising four dead leaders of Athens, succeeded and that these leaders are being formally honoured in the city, perhaps in the same manner as Peace in this comedy.

The structure of *Peace*

As suggested in the last chapter, 'farce' might be a better word for an Aristophanic comedy than 'drama'. Of the extant eleven plays only *Women at the Festival* has what we would consider a linear plot with a beginning, complications and a resolution at the end. While most of the Aristophanic comedies that we possess are rather loosely constructed, they do display a series of repeated elements which the spectators would be expecting. The following scheme is honoured more in the breach than in the observance, but it will be useful to set down these familiar elements of an Old Comedy. There is no 'typical' Aristophanic comedy; the closest we get to the sequence listed below are *Knights* and *Wasps*. There is considerable evidence in the remains of the other comic poets for the use of similar structural units (a *parabasis* at F 99 of Eupolis' *Demes*, a choral *parodos* at F 171 of Cratinus' *Wealth-Gods*, and two lines from an *agōn* in Eupolis' *Autolycus* (F 60). But it seems that these poets could employ these structural units in different ways – Eupolis F 205 (*Maricas*) suggests that Eupolis opened his play with a direct address to the spectators, and not in the usual iambic metre.

A comedy opens with a **prologue**, often in several scenes and considerably longer than in tragedy. The metre is principally the iambic trimeter, the basic metre of Greek drama, which Aristotle described as 'most like that of speech' (*Poetics* 1449a24). Here the poet warms up the audience, identifies the principal characters and chorus, and presents the great idea that will lie at the heart of the comedy. A character in Antiphanes' fourth-century comedy *Poetry* (F 189) complains that tragic poets have it easy since the details of tragic stories are well-known to all, but 'it's not the same for us. We must invent everything, new names ... what happened before, what's going on now, the ending, the prologue.' A common opening involves a pair of speaking characters: slaves as in *Knights, Wasps* and *Peace,* a master and slave (*Frogs, Wealth*), two Athenians seeking a new life (*Birds*), a father and son (*Clouds*), or Euripides and his relative by marriage (*Women at the Festival*). Alternatively, one character can deliver a soliloquy and then be joined by other speaking characters (*Acharnians, Lysistrata, Women at the Assembly*). Comic prologues usually run on for several scenes. *Peace* opens with two complaining slaves preparing cakes of excrement for the ravenous dung-beetle, but when that joke runs dry at line 49, the action shifts to the explanation of the great idea (50–81), then the appearance and flight of Trygaeus on the dung-beetle (82–178), next his arrival on Olympus and encounter with Hermes (178–235), and finally the scene with War and Riot which ends with Trygaeus' new plan to achieve peace (236–300).

The formal entry of the chorus is called the **parodos** ('way on', 'entrance'). Sometimes they rush on in haste (*Acharnians, Knights*), sometimes summoned by a character (*Clouds, Peace, Birds, Lysistrata, Women at the Assembly, Wealth*), sometimes as part of their normal routine (*Wasps, Frogs*). *Choros* in Greek meant 'dancing group', and much of the entertainment will have been the visual dance routines, especially in *Peace* where the chorus cannot stop dancing for joy at the prospect of peace (318–36). The metre used at 301–45 is the usual trochaic tetrameter catalectic,[1] a metre of excitement used when the chorus enters quickly and aggressively, especially so at *Ach.* 203–36 and

Kn. 247–83. In some plays the chorus enters as an opponent (*Acharnians, Wasps, Birds*), in others as a supporter of the great idea (*Knights, Lysistrata, Women at the Assembly, Wealth*), and in others as a spectator (*Frogs*). In *Peace* they are on Trygaeus' side from the moment that he summons them 'to pull out Peace who is loved by all' (292–300).

This entry of the chorus is often followed by some loosely structured scenes where the two sides confront each other, often with insults and physical threats. It is sometimes called a **pre-*agōn*** when it leads into the formal one-on-one confrontation (***agōn***) where the great idea is debated and realized. These scenes are marked by a fast and furious exchange of one-liners between opposing characters, especially true in *Knights* (273–301) and *Wasps* (415–525). In *Peace*, the only such skirmish occurs at 361–432 when Hermes comes out to threaten Trygaeus and the chorus with the wrath of Zeus if they persist in their attempt to rescue Peace, but he easily succumbs to the offer of a bribe – 'I have always been fond of gold' (425).

At this point in a comedy there should follow the ***agōn*** ('struggle', 'contest'). In Aristophanes this was a formally structured scene, where one opponent and then the other argued their case, always in the presence of the chorus and often with a third-party as observer or arbiter (the son in *Clouds*, Tereus in *Birds*, Dionysus in *Frogs*). In its full form an *agōn* would begin with a song by the chorus and introduction of the first speaker. The first speaker makes his or her case in an **epirrhēma** ('speech'), which can be interrupted by a character or the chorus. It is presented in an elevated metre (iambic or anapaestic tetrameters catalectic) and ending with the same metre reduced to dimeters. This last part was known as a **pnigos** or 'choking song', which may have been performed in a single breath like the conclusion of a patter song in Gilbert and Sullivan. Sometimes the *pnigos* may be a dialogue between the antagonists or (as at *Frogs* 971–91, 1077–98) between the speaker and a third party, but equally often the speaker slides easily from his tetrameters to dimeters without interruption. This same structure is repeated for the second speaker, and the *agōn* ends with a coda by the chorus. The anapaestic tetrameter catalectic is a lofty and dignified metre, called the 'Aristophanean' by the ancients, while the iambic tetrameter catalectic is more prosaic. It is worth noting that in the *agōnes* of *Clouds* and *Frogs* the older and more serious figure speaks in anapaests and his modern and (too) clever opponent uses iambics.

Of the extant eleven plays *Clouds* and *Knights* have two *agōnes* of the form described above, *Wasps, Frogs, Lysistrata,* and *Wealth* a single one. Here the two speakers outline the great idea and a decision is made, sometimes through persuasion, sometimes through force of arms. Normally, the second speaker is victorious, which may have had consequences for dramatic structure and the spectators' suspense, but in *Wealth* Poverty speaks second and has the better of the argument. Yet that comedy proceeds as if the first speaker (Chremylus) had won. He merely dismisses Poverty with the words 'Piss off and don't utter another syllable, for you won't persuade me even if you did!' (598–600). In two other comedies (*Birds, Women at the Assembly*) we have the formal structure of an *agōn,* but with no opposing speaker. The main characters (Peisetaerus, Praxagora) present a two-part exposition of their great ideas to other characters and the chorus. In both cases someone has to be persuaded, but there no one argues formally the opposing case. In two further comedies (*Acharnians, Women at the Festival*) a speaker presents a detailed argument to a hostile chorus, but neither speaks in an elevated metre, only in the normal iambic trimeters, and the formal structure of the *agōn* is completely absent.

Peace is the only extant comedy without a formal *agōn* or any real conflict. This has caused unsympathetic critics to conclude that there is no real drama, nothing like the pleas of Dicaeopolis in *Acharnians* for peace, no opponent to be debated and overcome, just a sustained note of festive exuberance. In the prologue, Trygaeus' quest is to confront Zeus, an encounter that never occurs. In a subsequent scene we meet War, a monstrous figure, and in a satyr-drama he would be a worthy antagonist to be defeated. But War and Riot get one scene (236–88) and then vanish from the play. The only conflicts are first those with Hermes, first at the doorway to Olympus (179–235) and later when they begin the rescue of Peace (361–425), and then the apparent dissension within the choral ranks. But these are hardly in the same league as the violent confrontations in other comedies or the frightening monster in satyr-drama. Some have tried to find the equivalent of an *agōn* in the two scenes in trochaic tetrameters catalectic that follow the rescue of Peace (553–81, 601–56), an unusual metre for an actors' scene in Old Comedy, but there is little confrontation here, only an explanation of previous events.

The *agōn* is often followed by an **episode** in the usual iambic trimeter. The best-known is the brilliant trial of the dogs in *Wasps* (835–1008), where Philocleon judges his first case at home, that against a house-dog (Labes – 'Snatcher') who has allegedly stolen and devoured a large Sicilian cheese. He is prosecuted by another dog (Cyon – 'Dog'); these names are slightly altered from those of two prominent political leaders, Laches and Cleon. Sometimes this episode is just a short transition from the high drama of the *agōn* (as at *Birds* 638–75) in which the actors prepare to leave the scene to the chorus. In *Peace* 657–728, this episode is rather longer and has Peace asking Hermes what has happened at Athens during her absence. This sets up a familiar feature of Aristophanic comedy, a thematic sequence of personal jokes. The first two are political, aimed at Cleonymus (670–8), the 'greatest friend of peace' since he allegedly threw his shield away in battle, and Hyperbolus, 'who now rules on the Pnyx' (679–92). Being a lamp-dealer he will be able to enlighten the city. They then switch to jokes about dramatists, an obscure reference to the tragedian Sophocles (695–9) and then an inquiry about Cratinus, the senior comic poet, who died 'when the Laconians invaded ... because he couldn't bear seeing a full jar of wine destroyed'. Cratinus as the senile drunkard was a running joke over a number of comedies. The scene finishes quickly with the departure of Trygaeus and the handmaidens of Peace and the playing-area left to the chorus. The dung-beetle has already vanished to draw the chariot of Zeus.

There now follows one of the distinctive features of Old Comedy, the **parabasis**. The verb *parabainein* can mean 'to step forward', and becomes a technical term for the comic chorus 'coming forward' to address the spectators – 'if any comic poet would come forward (*parabas*) and sing his own praises to the audience in the anapaests' (*Peace* 734–5). Like the *agōn*, the *parabasis* in Aristophanes has a distinctive sub-structure, although not every *parabasis* will possess all of these features – the most 'typical' is that at *Wasps* 1009–1121. Aristophanes' last two extant comedies, *Women at the Assembly* and *Wealth*, have no *parabasis* at all.

In its full form, the *parabasis* will begin with a short song by the chorus – this is lacking in *Peace*. The chorus then turn to 'the anapaests' (or **parabasis proper**), a lengthy section in the elevated anapaestic tetrameters catalectic, which as in the *agōn* can be cut in half and end with a *pnigos* in anapaestic dimeters (*Peace* 729–73). In the comedies of the 420s the chorus abandons its dramatic identity and speaks in the anapaests for the comic poet – at *Peace* 754 slipping into the first person singular ('I fight for all'). Their subject is not the events of the play or their dramatic character, but an *apologia* for the poet's art and a denigration of his rivals. In the anapaests of *Birds* and *Women at the Festival*, the chorus remain in their dramatic character and do not break the dramatic illusion. An unusual aspect of the anapaests in *Peace* is that Aristophanes repeats lines from *Wasps* (*Wasps* 1029–35 ~ *Peace* 754–9), where he compares himself to Heracles and his enemy Cleon to a fearsome monster.

The rest of the *parabasis* consists of a four-part structure known formally as an **epirrhematic syzygy**: a song (**ode**), formal speech (*epirrhēma*), song (**antode**), formal speech (*antepirrhēma*). The metre of the *epirrhēmata* is the trochaic tetrameter catalectic, a faster-paced metre without the loftiness of the anapaests or the prosaic tone of the iambic tetrameter. The chorus return to their dramatic character and explain the life of a cavalryman (*Knights*), why aged jurors should appear as wasps (*Wasps*), or what life in the sky is like (*Birds*). The *parabasis* of *Peace* is unusual in two ways. First the *parabasis* lacks both epirrhematic sections and consists only of the anapaests (729–73), the ode (774–95), and the antode (796–816). There are parallels for truncated *parabases*, as in *Women at the Festival* we find only the anapaests (785–829) and one *epirrhēma* (830–45), and in *Frogs* the anapaests have been moved from the *parabasis* to the *parodos* (354–71). At *Peace* 553–81 and 601–56 we have a pair of scenes in trochaic tetrameter catalectic, the first hailing the arrival of Peace and the second explaining how the War began. Has Aristophanes perhaps removed the trochaic *epirrhēmata* from the *parabasis* and placed them earlier in the play? These two scenes, however, are much longer than the *epirrhēmata* of the *parabasis*, which tend to be sixteen or twenty lines at most. Second, in the lyrics the chorus do not sing as farmers, but as dramatic spectators who invoke not Peace, but a Muse. They sing in honour of 'the great poet' and pray not to endure the efforts of Carcinus and his sons, Morsimus or Melanthius, inferior tragic performers who are described in a series of bizarre and imaginative epithets.

The second half of an Aristophanic comedy tends to be a loose assemblage of **episodes** separated by songs. The principal exception is *Frogs*, where the episodes occur in the first part of the comedy and the *agōn* is delayed so that the play may end with the decision of whether Aeschylus or Euripides is the better tragedian. Usually, the episodes show the (il)logical consequences of the great idea, as various characters enter to comment on, oppose, or to exploit the new order. These are often called 'intruder scenes' where the main character dispatches unwelcome guests with abusive language and comic violence. The episodes in *Peace* consist of Trygaeus' return to his home (819–55), the handing over of Holiday to the Council (868–909), the formal installation of Peace (923–1022), and the arrival of the oracle-monger Hierocles (1045–1126) seeking to crash the sacrificial feast.

The choral interludes are mostly short, but one can fairly be described as a **second *parabasis***, since it repeats the epirrhematic structure of the principal *parabasis*. In *Peace* this occurs at lines 1127–90 and contains some of the most appealing poetry in Aristophanes, where the chorus of farmers indulge in an emotional and lyrical vision of the delights of the countryside in peacetime. In two brief episodes after the second *parabasis* Trygaeus welcomes a sickle-seller (an agricultural implement) and deals with an arms-dealer, turning his implements of war to other uses (1191–1264). Two boys come out to sing (1265–1315), the son of Lamachus chanting martial lines from Homer and the son of Cleonymus (an alleged coward) a poem from Archilochus about throwing one's shield away in combat (F 5). The closing scene in a comedy is known as the *exodos* ('departure'). Here Trygaeus sings a song for his wedding to Harvest (1316–31) and the chorus celebrate their union in sexually suggestive language. Trygaeus closes the comedy by promising, 'if you people follow me, you will be eating cakes', presumably of a different sort from the dung-balls prepared in the prologue.

The chorus in *Peace*

The speaker of Antiphanes F 189 quoted above complains that a comic poet has to work harder than a tragic poet, since he must make up all of the characters and the action out of new cloth. One of these tasks is to introduce the chorus of his comedy before they actually make their way onto the scene. In tragedy, the myth would narrow down the potential identity of a chorus, but in the fantastic world of an Aristophanic comedy anything is possible. In each of the eleven extant comedies the spectators learn the identity of the chorus before they enter, often with a hint of how they will interact with the events being enacted: hostile Acharnians, sympathetic cavalrymen etc. Trygaeus' initial summons seems to call more than farmers to assist in the rescue of Peace: 'Farmers, merchants, builders and craftsmen, metics and visitors and men from the islands, all of you come here as quick as you can, with your shovels and crowbars and ropes' (296–8). But throughout the comedy their identity seems to fluctuate. At first Trygaeus is thinking about Greece as a whole (59, 93, 105–8, 408), and is appalled at War's threat to make a savoury-mash out of various Greek states, not just Athens. Trygaeus' initial appeal at 292 is to 'men of Greece', but the reference at 297–8 to 'metics and visitors and men from the islands' reveals an Athenian setting.[2] At 302, the chorus describe themselves as 'all Greeks' (*Panhellenes*), but at 346–59 the chorus recall 'the many hardships and bivouacs that I endured, which are the preserve of Phormion'. Since Phormion was a successful Athenian general, this makes it a specifically Athenian context, as do the references to the Lyceum and the Athenian leader Peisander (395).

In the rescue scene (459–519), the singling out of certain sub-groups reinforces the Panhellenic composition of the chorus: Boeotians (466), Spartans (478), Megarians (481), Argives (493). At 496–507, Hermes asks certain ill-minded (*kakonooi*) persons to stop hindering the rescue of Peace and in fact to leave the scene. Specifically mentioned are the Megarians, who are blamed elsewhere for causing the War (*Ach.* 515–38, *Peace* 608–10), and those Athenians who prefer litigation to peace. By 508–11 we are left with the farmers (*geōrgoi*) as 'the only ones who are pulling the job off'. If there were distinctive sub-units in this larger group, how would these be indicated? Elsewhere in Aristophanes, ethnic distinction is indicated by a comically distorted dialect (Persian, Megarian and Theban in *Acharnians*, Spartan in *Lysistrata*), but the chorus in this section of *Peace* speaks and sings in good Attic Greek. And how would Athenian farmers be distinguished from the other Athenians who prefer life in the law-courts? Did these last enter without the requisite tools that Trygaeus requested at line 299?

It is unlikely that more than the usual twenty-four chorus members responded to Trygaeus' call and that this number was winnowed down to twenty-four Athenian farmers as the others were dismissed. Groups of 'extras' are documented in both tragedy and comedy: the children in Euripides' *Children of Heracles*, the Athenian citizens in *Eumenides*, the crowd of slaves and citizens at the end of *Lysistrata*. But these are entities separate from the principal chorus and there is no parallel for a larger-than-usual chorus being reduced to normal size during the course of the drama. Alternatively, a double chorus has been suggested: twelve Panhellenes and twelve Athenian farmers. We have examples of divided choruses in extant comedy. At *Ach.* 557–72, the chorus splits after Dicaeopolis finishes his speech, some in support and some unmoved, but by 626 they reunite. In *Lysistrata* there are two half-choruses throughout, of old men and old women and again they reconcile by

1042, and we know that Eupolis' *Maricas* also had a chorus of the rich and another of poor people, who came together at F 192.29. But *Peace* could hardly have continued with only a half-chorus. Platnauer (1964: 95) dismisses these extras as 'mere creatures of the imagination' while Sommerstein (1985: xviii–xix, 156) argues that '*something* happened to the chorus just before 508', but there was no actual reduction – 'this might have been contrived ... by concentrating the same number of *choreutae* in a smaller space.'

The problem is due in part to the modern expectation that if something is indicated in the words of the play, then an actual visual event corresponded to what was said. Taplin (1978) argued that any stage directions that have come down to us in the tradition are not genuine and that all we need to recreate the action are the words of the text. But the opposite may not necessarily be true, that all words in the text were actually enacted out before the spectators. Describing Greek tragedy as 'theatre of the mind',[3] he argued that the spectators relied heavily on their own imagination to supply the details in what was essentially minimalist theatre. Menander's later comedy *The Grouch* (316) opens with the instruction, 'imagine that the setting is Phyle in Attica', and there are more than a few places where a change of scene is suggested in the text, but it is likely that no overt scenic changes were made. In *Libation-Bearers* by Aeschylus the first half is played at the tomb in the centre of the *orchēstra*, the second before the door of the palace. In each case the spectators will have ignored the other part of the visual scene before them. In the following play *Eumenides*, the first scenes take place at the door of the temple of Apollo at Delphi, while the next part is focused around the statue of Athena in the centre. We are too used to the theatre of realism to appreciate how a theatre of the imagination operated.

The identity of the chorus continues to fluctuate for the rest of the drama. During the song at 582–600 they sing as 'country-folk [*agroikoi*] who live a farmer's life'. There are no specific local references, but the natural assumption is that it is the Attic countryside they are longing for. In the *parabasis* nothing marks them out as farmers, unlike earlier plays such as *Acharnians, Knights* and *Wasps* where the chorus' identity is developed through much of the *parabasis*. Here they are spectators at the Athenian dramatic festivals, and explain why their poet is the one 'who has become the best and most famous comic producer' (736–7), by claiming that he has risen above the inferior and unoriginal comedy of his rivals and built up a great art with his excellent jokes. They repeat a striking passage from the *parabasis* of *Wasps* (1029–37 ~ *Peace* 752–60), where Aristophanes compares himself to Heracles and his enemy Cleon to a monster to be vanquished.[4] The *parabasis* proper ends with an appeal to 'honour the bald man' – Aristophanes seems to be either prematurely bald or with a distinctly receding forehead – and a description of him as 'the noblest of poets' (773). As stated above, the *parabasis* of *Peace* lacks the trochaic *epirrhēmata* and contains only an ode and antode, both of which continue the theatrical theme with imaginative attacks on current dramatic performers, first Carcinus and his sons who, it seems, had danced poorly in the closing scenes of *Wasps* the previous year, and then Morsimus and Melanthius, two inferior tragic poets.

The chorus has little to do in the scenes that follow the *parabasis*. They have two pairs of choral dialogue (856–67 ~ 910–21 and 939–55 ~ 1023–38) where they sing in lyrics and Trygaeus replies in iambic trimeter, but this middle third of the comedy is dominated by Trygaeus and his slave. At 556–600, the chorus joined in the lyric celebration of the rescue of Peace, but here the anapaestic dimeters that follow the installation of Peace (974–1015) are sung by Trygaeus and the slave.[5] It is in the second *parabasis* that the chorus' character as Athenian farmers emerges most strongly. Aristophanes' characters constantly balance the delights of the countryside with the troubles of life in the city – a frequent word for the latter is *pragmata* ('matters'), which has the negative sense of 'troubles' and 'bother'. Dicaeopolis sings how his private peace has made him 'free from troubles and battles and Lamachus' (*Ach.* 269–70).[6] When Trygaeus introduces himself at *Peace* 191, he claims to be 'no informer nor lover of troubles', and the chorus greets the prospect of peace at 346–8, 'I wish that I could see that day, since I have endured many troubles.' The chorus sums up well the change from war to peace in the ode (1127–39):

> I am happy, so happy, to be rid of helmets, of cheese and onions. For I take no pleasure in battles, but in drinking down wine with good friends, kindling a fire from logs that have dried well over the summer, roasting some chickpeas and grilling acorns, kissing the slave-girl while my wife is in the bath.

In the *parabases* proper of the comedies of the 420s, including the partially revised *Clouds c.* 419/18, the chorus drops its dramatic identity and speaks openly for the comic poet. There is little, if any, hint that they are elderly charcoal-burners from Acharnae or jurors in the guise of wasps. They may resume those identities in the epirrhematic sections of the *parabasis*, but for the *parabasis* proper they have become solely participants in the drama with a point to make about comedy. Throughout the *parabasis* proper of *Clouds* (518–62) they speak in the first-person singular as the offended poet defends his creation, and at *Peace* 754 they slide from the third person to *machomai* ('I fight') and remain as 'I' until the end of the *parabasis* proper: 'show me your gratitude' (761), 'be on my side' (765), 'when I win' (769). When the chorus first appear in *Frogs* (316–459), they are initiates in the underworld and their *parodos* is an extended comic parody of a ritual song. In the *parabasis* (674–737), however, they begin in a plural voice but soon switch to the singular '*I* say' (692), and is that 'I' the poet or his chorus? When they call themselves 'the sacred chorus' at 686, are they singing in their dramatic role as initiates or as performers in a comedy performed at a festival of Dionysus? For the rest of *Frogs* they assume the role of dramatic spectators. What is noteworthy about *Peace* is that the fluctuation in their choral identity begins early, during the rescue of Peace, and that the *parabasis* lacks the epirrhematic sections, where the chorus might have reverted to their original personality. Here too they are involved spectators of the dramatic competitions. In *Frogs*, the initiates have their great moment in the *parodos*, for the farmers in *Peace* it comes in the second *parabasis* (1127–90), where they express their joy at the end of war and the resumption of the pleasant life in the country.

The structure of *Peace*

Prologue (1–300): (i) 1–49, two slaves; (ii) 50–61, monologue by a slave; (iii) 62–179, the flight of Trygaeus; (iv) 180–235, Hermes and Trygaeus; (v) 236–300, War and Riot.

Parodos (301–60).

Episodes (361–728): (i) 361–458, Hermes and Trygaeus; (ii) 459–519, the rescue of Peace; (iii) 520–600, the welcome of Peace; (iv) 601–57, how the war began; (v) 657–728, Peace's questions.

Parabasis (729–816): (i) 729–73, the anapaests; (ii) 774–95, ode; (iii) 796–816, antode.

Episodes (819–1125): (i) 819–55, Trygaeus and his slave; (ii) 856–67, chorus; (iii) 868–909, Theoria; (iv) 910–21, chorus; (v) 922–1022, the installation of Peace; (vi) 1023–38, chorus; (vii) 1039–1125, Hierocles the intruder.

Second *Parabasis* (1127–90): (i) 1127–39, ode; (ii) 1140–58, *epirrhēma*; (iii) 1159–71, antode; (iv) 1172–90, *antepirrhēma*.

Episodes (1191–1304): (i) 1191–1264, Trygaeus and the arms-dealer; (ii) 1265–1304, Trygaeus and the two boys.

Exodos (1305–59).

Peace and its Historical Background

Ancient writers saw a direct connection between the democracy at Athens and the freedom of expression in Old Comedy. The otherwise unknown writer Platonius writes:

> In the time of Aristophanes and Cratinus and Eupolis democracy ruled at Athens where the people possessed supreme authority, being lords and masters of political affairs. Since all enjoyed freedom of speech, the writers of comedy were not afraid of poking fun at generals and jurors who gave bad verdicts, and at any of the citizens who were hungry for money or lived a corrupt life. As I have observed, the people removed any fear on the part of the comic poets because they were eager to hear them insult such men, and we do know that the people were fundamentally and innately hostile to the rich and enjoyed their discomfitures. So then in the time of Aristophanes and Cratinus and Eupolis the comic poets were a powerful force against wrong-doers.
>
> Koster I.2–13

Platonius and other ancient writers considered most Old Comedy to be such a blend of a topical theme and personal satire, but this was really one aspect of the larger genre and was in vogue principally in the years 430–400. It was these comic poets, especially the familiar triad of Cratinus, Eupolis and Aristophanes, and their political and personally abusive comedy that attracted the attention of ancient and modern students of the genre.

For Aristophanes, the *polis* of Athens lies at the heart of his comedies. Of his plays from the 420s *Acharnians* is, like *Peace*, about making peace with Sparta as one man (Dicaeopolis) defies his city and makes his own personal treaty. *Knights* and *Wasps* both deal with political institutions of the city, the popular assembly (*Knights*) and the law courts (*Wasps*), and how these are manipulated by dishonest politicians such as Cleon. Political too were certain of the lost comedies of the 420s. We are told by the author of the third hypothesis to *Peace* that *Merchant-Ships*, probably performed at the Lenaea of 423, championed the cause of peace and made fun of Cleon and Lamachus as 'hawks'. The fragments of *Farmers* (see Appendix) similarly suggest a comedy about war and peace, and his *Babylonians* (Dionysia of 426) contained something about Athens and the allies that offended Cleon and also showed Dionysus encountering a political informer. Plays of the topical-political sort are closely wedded to specific times, peoples and events, so much so that we can assign dates to both complete and fragmentary dramas based on contemporary references. For example, if we did not know the date of Aristophanes' *Knights* (Lenaea of 424), we would be able to date it between the events at Pylos (summer of 425) and the death of Cleon (autumn of 422). Similarly, Hermippus F 47 (*Fates*), which chides Pericles for his failure to prosecute the war, must belong to after the outbreak of war in May 431 and before Pericles' death from the plague in late 429, in other words to a festival in either 430 or 429.

Comedy and the Peloponnesian War

What we call the 'Peloponnesian War' was fought with interruptions between Athens and her allies and the Peloponnesian League led by Sparta from 431 to 404. We are fortunate in having a contemporary account for much of the conflict in the Athenian historian Thucydides. His family had property and connections in the North and he himself served as a general in a campaign in the North. He describes the authority of his histories in the opening of the fifth book which covers the negotiations which led to the peace with Sparta in 421:

> I lived throughout the whole of the war, old enough to understand matters, and paid close attention so that my knowledge would be accurate. It happened that I had to flee my own country for twenty years after my command at Amphipolis [424/3] and that by becoming

acquainted with events on both sides, especially the Peloponnesians because of my exile, I was able to be better informed of what took place.

5.26.5[1]

Thucydides (5.20) records that the first part of the Peloponnesian War lasted 'for ten years and a few days', by our reckoning (431–421). We have come to call this the 'Archidamian War', named for the Spartan king Archidamos who led the first invasion into Attica in the early summer of 431. Hostilities between Athens and Sparta had been brewing since the Persian invaders were driven from Greece in 479 and their wartime solidarity dissolved as both sides contended for primacy among the Greek states. Aristophanes looks back to this alliance of Athens and Sparta through a nostalgically rosy lens, especially at the end of *Lysistrata* where Athenians and Spartans come together to end their current war and revel in the past glory of their defeat of the Persians.

Supporting Athens and Sparta were organized leagues of allied states. When Sparta and her allies had by 470 withdrawn from the Hellenic League that was established to guard against future threats from Persia, the Athenians found themselves leading the remaining cities, principally those in and around the Aegean Sea. Called initially the 'Delian League' from its headquarters on the sacred island of Delos, its member-states supplied first ships and later funds to maintain a permanent naval defence force. But when in the 450s the league's treasury was moved to Athens, the alliance of free city-states became effectively a tribute-paying Athenian 'empire'. In comedy these are called 'the allies' (*Ach.* 506, *Cl.* 609, *Wasps* 673, *Peace* 639), or 'the islands' (*Cl.* 1034, 1319; *Peace* 298, 760), while at *Wasps* 707 Bdelycleon speaks of 'the thousand cities [*poleis*] which pay tribute to us' and at *Peace* 619 Hermes refers to 'the cities which you rule'. Eupolis' lost comedy *Cities* (*Poleis*) had a chorus of personified states from this alliance.[2]

The Spartans for their part presided over a formally organized group of allies, called the 'Peloponnesian League', whose origins went back to the sixth century. These were not in a tributary relationship with Sparta, nor could Sparta commit them to military action without their consent (Thuc. 1.118–19). After rapprochement with Athens yielded to hostility in the 470s, the principal concern of this league became how to counter the growing power of Athens. Sparta's principal allies outside of the Peloponnese were Corinth, Thebes and Megara, all of which lay geographically close to Athens and had reason to fear her naval and economic power. Much of the first book of Thucydides' history describes how Sparta's allies were the driving force in persuading her to go to war with Athens.

Earlier hostilities between Athens and Sparta (459–446), sometimes called the 'First Peloponnesian War', had to do more with Athenian actions against Sparta's allies, and only in 446 was there an actual Spartan incursion into Attica (Thuc. 1.114). The Spartan king Pleistoanax withdrew his forces swiftly and mysteriously, perhaps to be explained by the record of an expenditure by Pericles of ten talents 'for a necessary purpose' (*Clouds* 859). In 446/5 an official peace treaty aimed to last thirty years established zones of influence for both Sparta and Athens, but this lasted for only fifteen years. Although incidents at Corcyra and Potidaea (late 430s) brought Athens and Corinth into open conflict, Thucydides (1.23.6, 1.118) maintains that 'the real cause of the war' was fear on the Spartan side of the growing power of Athens and that this fear was fostered by major allies of Sparta such as Corinth, Thebes and Megara. Sparta was less than enthusiastic about resuming active hostilities, but eventually yielded to pressure from her allies, especially Corinth (e.g., at 1.67–88). Both Andocides (3.8) and Aristophanes (*Ach.* 513–38, *Peace* 605–14) also consider as a principal *casus belli* an Athenian decree in the late 430s that placed a trade embargo on Megara within their sphere of influence. This had serious consequences for the Megarians, who appealed to Sparta for aid in rescinding that decree. At *Ach.* 535 they are described as 'gradually dying of hunger' and in the same play (729–835) Aristophanes rather cruelly brings on stage a starving Megarian willing to sell his daughters to get money for food. In *Peace*, Hermes likewise shows no sympathy for the Megarians who are imagined as being part of the chorus:

TRYG. But the Megarians aren't doing anything. And yet they are still pulling with all their might, grimacing like puppy dogs.

HERMES. Well, they are half-dead with starvation.

481–3

HERMES. Megarians, why don't you go to hell? The goddess has a long memory and hates you because you were the first to smear her with garlic.[3]

500–2

The strategies of the Archidamian War can be simply put. Spartan forces would prevail in a pitched land battle. Thus, they planned to invade Attica each year, destroy crops and fruit trees, and attempt to force the Athenians into a land engagement. They would also concentrate on dislodging Athens' allies from the 'empire'. The Athenians dominated the seas and could launch hit-and-run raids on Spartan territories in the Peloponnese. They had huge financial resources, their navy could keep the sea-routes open for needed supplies, and their city walls could protect them from a land attack. Accordingly, they evacuated the countryside and moved their rural population into the city, causing considerable hardship and discontent. Dicaeopolis opens *Acharnians* in the city, 'looking out to the countryside, in love with peace, hating the city, longing for my deme' (32–3). At 512 he adds that 'my vines have been cut down too'. The Sausage-Seller in *Knights* answers the claim of Paphlagon (a coded name for Cleon, a contemporary demagogue) to 'love the People' with the question, 'how is it loving him when you have seen him living in barrels and alleyways and attics for eight years now and feel no pity, just keep him locked up and fleece him?' (792–4). Hermes observes that 'when the working folk came in from the countryside, they did not realise that they too were being sold out' (*Peace* 632–3). The residents of the large and important deme of Acharnae strongly opposed Pericles' policy of *Sitzkrieg* and repeatedly demanded action against the Spartan invaders (Thuc. 2.19–22). These short-tempered and aggressive Acharnians form the chorus of Aristophanes' first extant comedy, who oppose Dicaeopolis' private peace with Sparta.

Thucydides' account of the first year of the war (2.18–32) exemplifies the tactics on both sides. The Spartans invaded Attica in the early summer, destroyed crops and vines and fruit trees, and after trying unsuccessfully to provoke the Athenians into an open encounter, withdrew back to their own country. The Athenians responded with damaging hit-and-run naval raids around the Peloponnese and with attempts to shore up their influence in the North. If neither side could win an all-out victory, Athens would be the *de facto* winner, since the Spartan pretext for the War was to check the growth of Athens' power and 'liberate' the allies from the 'tyranny' of Athens. Thus, the Spartans expended considerable effort in trying to detach the allies from Athens' imperial control and to undermine Athens' use of the mining and timber resources in the North.

Both sides miscalculated their larger strategies. By bringing a large population into the restricted confines of the city, the Athenians were open to the disastrous effects of a plague which broke out in 430 with further outbreaks over the next few years (Thuc. 2.47–54). Casualties were considerable, sometimes estimated at one-quarter to one-third of the Athenian military, and included their leader Pericles, who died late in 429, as well as damaging their overall morale. The Athenians also underestimated the Spartan ability to dislodge disaffected allies from the Athenian 'empire', the most prominent being the major cities on Lesbos who revolted briefly in 427. The potential peril of conflicts on land was proven too true when an over-confident Athenian force engaged the Thebans at Delion with unfortunate results in the late summer of 424. They were also surprised by the Spartan leader Brasidas who marched his army the length of Greece to attack Athenian interests in the North. The Spartans, on their side, did not appreciate how damaging the naval raids by the Athenians could be and were completely dismayed when a Spartan military force was first trapped and then captured on the island of Sphacteria near Pylos on the west coast in 425. In *Knights* (424-L) Paphlagon (Cleon) boasts loudly of his victory. Pylos became a fortified Athenian base in enemy territory and caused much damage to Spartan morale. The Spartan incursions into Attica ceased and both Thucydides and Aristophanes record that the Spartans made several peace overtures in order to regain these captives. At *Kn.* 794–5 the Sausage-Seller claims that 'when Archeptolemus offered Peace you totally rejected him,' and at *Peace* 665–7 Hermes reports that 'after the Pylos business she says she came of her own free will bearing a chest full of truces and was rejected three times in the assembly'.[4]

Peace and the peace negotiations

Athenian loss of morale over their defeat at Delion and their fears about Brasidas' activities in the North combined with Sparta's concern for those captured at Pylos caused both sides and their allies to conclude a one-year truce for 423/2 (Thuc. 4.117–18). In Thucydides' view there were expectations that this would lead to a more permanent peace and when the truce expired in the summer of 422, it took two months before military action resumed. Principally because affairs in the North were unsettled and still of great concern to Athens, Cleon himself proposed and led the expeditionary force in a campaign to maintain their hold on the allies in the region (Thuc. 5.2–11). The end result was a military engagement at Amphipolis (probably in mid-October), where the Spartans under Brasidas won a striking victory, but both he and Cleon perished in the fighting.

Thucydides and Aristophanes agree that the events at Amphipolis opened the way for serious peace negotiations, 'since both Cleon and Brasidas had been killed – and they were the ones on either side especially opposed to peace' (Thuc. 5.16). In *Peace*, War does not name them as the pestles that he needs to grind up the cities of Greece into a paste (259–88), but line 270 clearly identifies one as Cleon, 'the leather merchant who used to stir up Greece', and in lines 283–4 the Spartans lost their pestle (Brasidas) 'by loaning it to some people in the region of Thrace'. Thucydides (5.14) sums up the motives on both sides. The Athenians were now dismayed at this further defeat at Amphipolis, and the loss of their previous confidence was coupled with a growing concern about the loyalties of the cities within their 'empire'. The Spartans for their part now realized that their strategy of bringing down Athenian power by yearly invasions of Attica had not worked and the disaster at Pylos led to the capture of Spartan troops and the establishment of an Athenian base in their territory. They feared also a revolt of their helot (slave) population and the approaching expiry of their truce with their local rival in the Peloponnese, Argos, presented the dangerous possibility of a war on two fronts.

Thucydides identifies a leading figure on each side, the Spartan king Pleistoanax and the Athenian general Nicias,[5] and assigns to them personal motives for pursuing the peace negotiations. Nicias' alleged motive is to pass on to posterity a reputation for never having harmed the state, this best accomplished by keeping it out of danger, since 'it was peace that guaranteed freedom from peril' (5.16.1). Pleistoanax, Thucydides alleges, was anxious to deflect attention from previous irregularities in his kingship, i.e. taking bribes, and 'since, as long as there was a state of war, it was inevitable that leading men would be attacked when things went badly, he was very keen on an agreement' (5.17). Hermes' summary of the origin of the conflict includes this revealing comment about both the Athenian allies and the Spartan leaders:

> and then when the cities which you ruled realized that you were at odds with and snarling at one another, they started plotting against you being afraid of the tribute and tried to win over the leaders of the Spartans with bribes. Being so fond of money and xenophobes to boot, they expelled this goddess in a disgraceful manner and took up with War instead.
>
> 619–24

Negotiations began in earnest after the battle at Amphipolis (mid-October 422) and continued through the winter (Thuc. 5.17.2). Thucydides (5.17) mentions that a principal stumbling-block was how territory lost during the war should be restored to either side and how certain cities, such as Amphipolis, Plataea and Nisaea, should be treated.

'Toward the spring', the Spartans seem to have upped the ante by threatening to create a permanent advanced position in Attica. This threat seems to have had the desired effect and a fifty-year peace treaty was concluded 'immediately after the City Dionysia'. Thucydides lists the articles of agreement at 5.18–19. Aspects of the peace process seem to make their way into the text of Aristophanes' comedy. These were negotiations between Athens and Sparta, with their respective allies having little to do with the process or the details. During the hauling-scene (459–519) various units of the chorus are dismissed for not doing their fair share of the work: the Boeotians (464–6), Megarians (481–3, 500–2) and Argives (491–3). Thucydides (5.22–4) records that at a meeting of the Peloponnesian League the Megarians, Corinthians, Boeotians and Elians refused to sign the peace accord and that after their return from signing the treaty at Athens the Spartans ordered their allies to accept the terms of that treaty, but they persisted in their refusal 'until they made a more equitable treaty'. Thus, their lack of enthusiasm was well-known enough for Aristophanes to incorporate it into the comedy. Also, the first clause in the treaty (Thuc. 5.18.1) ensures the freedom to visit the common sanctuaries of the Greeks; the Greek verb here is *theōrein* and the prominence of this issue in the negotiations may have been the inspiration for Peace's handmaid, Theoria.

Peace and the politicians (especially Cleon)

Athens in the fifth century, especially after the controversial reforms in the late 460s, was nominally a democracy, at least for adult citizen males, but her politics were dominated by leaders from the important families, who referred to themselves as the *aristoi* ('the best') or the *kaloi k'agathoi* ('fine and good'). It would be a mistake to think in terms of 'parties' organized around a political platform or philosophy. Critics of the last century talked blithely of 'the Peace Party' or 'the War Party', but politics were conducted around prominent men and their friends and were thus personality-centred rather than issue-based. Under a procedure called 'ostracism' a leading figure in the state could be exiled from Athens for ten years. Where modern democracies employ referenda to decide issues, the Athenians settled matters by removing a leader. There were, of course, issues that polarized the Athenian assembly, such as whether to pursue an aggressive policy against Persia and a rapprochement with Sparta (that of Cimon in the 460s) or the opposite course (favoured by Pericles). That issue was settled by the ostracism of Cimon in 461. The controversial reforms of the late 460s, which stripped the Areopagos Council of its traditional powers, led also to the assassination of Ephialtes, the principal proponent of these reforms. There existed also a definite opposition of 'democracy' as opposed to 'oligarchy' (or 'tyranny'). This is especially clear in Thucydides' account of the internal stasis at Corcyra (3.81–4), in a well-known debate from Euripides' play *Suppliant Women* (422?) between Theseus king of Athens and a herald from Thebes, where both sides score telling points, and in a pamphlet, perhaps from the 420s, attributed to Xenophon but whose author is generally called 'the Old Oligarch'. Here the author separates Athenians into 'the people' or 'the poor' or 'the inferior' as against 'the rich' and 'the decent', and presents Athenian political practice with a very jaundiced eye.

Pericles, connected on his mother's side with the noble family of the Alcmaeonidae, had been the leading political figure at Athens since the late 460s and had enjoyed an unchallenged position from the late 440s until the start of the Archidamian War. Any opposition to him had come from traditional conservative leaders such as Cimon and Thucydides son of Melesias (not the historian), both removed by the process of ostracism. But in the 420s a new force appeared in Athenian politics, the *dēmagōgoi*. The word means essentially 'leaders of the people', but it possessed the same pejorative overtones as 'demagogue' does today. If we were to believe the comic poets, these were illiterate and jumped-up tradesmen from the market-place, likely of foreign birth and thus not legitimate citizens, ill-educated and unable to speak good Attic Greek, dishonest and in politics for their own personal gain, the best demagogues having been rent-boys in their youth. They used flamboyant and aggressive verbal tactics in the assembly and exploited the law-courts as weapons against their political foes. In reality they were members of the commercial middle-class who had prospered greatly during the fifty years of Athens' military and economic ascendancy. Their trades included selling bran (Eucrates), dealing in sheep (Lysicles), tanning leather (Cleon) and lamp-making (Hyperbolus). Having achieved financial success – we know that Cleon's father was wealthy enough in the 450s to have served as a *chorēgos* – they naturally sought political power and public influence.

The first of these is Cleon, first mentioned by Hermippus as an aggressive opponent of Pericles in his comedy *Fates* (F 47) in 430 or 429. Thucydides (3.36–50) describes the part he played in the revolt of the cities on Lesbos in 427, including a speech set in his mouth criticizing the decision of the assembly not to execute the male citizens and enslave the women and children. His contemporaries Aristophanes and Thucydides deliberately set Cleon in a bad light. Thucydides describes him as 'not only a most violent person but also the most influential among the people at that time' (3.36.6), while Aristophanes writes an entire comedy (*Knights*) in which the *dēmos* ('the People') is presented as a house-owner and Cleon as a slave named 'Paphlagon', an epithet which suggests both foreign origin – Paphlagonian slaves were not uncommon at Athens – and a vocal mannerism, from *paphlazein* ('to splutter').[6] Cleon evidently had a distinctive speaking voice – see *Wasps* 31–41 where a slave has a dream about a monstrous sea-creature speaking to an assembly of sheep 'with a voice of a scalded sow'. Aristotle's summary of Cleon has further coloured our view of this leader (*Constitution of Athens* 28.3):

> the leader of the people was Cleon son of Cleaenetus who seems to have done the most to corrupt the people with his outbursts and was the first to gird up his cloak before making a public speech and to shout and use verbal abuse from the speaker's platform, when everyone else would speak with decorum.

Few ancient sources about Cleon present him in a positive light. But Aristophanes could tar-and-feather Cleon in his prize-winning *Knights*

at the Lenaea of 424 and then watch him be elected general some weeks
later. Comedy may not have made much of a political impact on its own
time, but it certainly affected the views of later critics.

Cleon was the favourite political target of Aristophanes and figures
in each of the first five extant comedies. In *Acharnians*, the poet
identifies himself with his chief character Dicaeopolis and complains of
some legal action taken by Cleon against him 'because of last year's
comedy' (377–82). This was Aristophanes' lost *Babylonians*, a political
comedy involving the Athenian allies, in which Aristophanes said
something that offended Cleon – remember that Cleon was deeply
involved in the debate over punishing the revolt of the allied cities on
Lesbos in 427. *Knights*, an entire comedy devoted to a personal and
political attack on Cleon, ends with the demagogue's overthrow and
the Athenian *dēmos* returned to the 'good old days', while in *Wasps* the
main characters are the father named 'Love Cleon' and his son called
'Loathe Cleon'. Cleon appears in the comedy as a dog (Cyon, 'dog')
prosecuting another dog (Labes, 'snatcher'), in a brilliant parody of an
Athenian trial.

Cleon was dead by the time of the production of *Peace*, and comedy
tends to leave a target alone after their death. A previous target can
acquire respect in death. Lamachus the bellicose 'hawk' of *Acharnians*
and *Peace* becomes an Athenian hero at *Women at the the Festival*
839–45 and *Frogs* 1039, while Pericles, who is the target of repeated
personal and political attacks by Cratinus, Hermippus and Aristophanes
(*Ach.* 526–37, *Peace* 603–18), is raised from the dead in Eupolis' *Demes*
(417) and hailed as a hero of the city. In *Peace*, Cleon is mentioned by
name only once (47–9); the rest of the time Aristophanes alludes to him
indirectly, as the 'leather-merchant' at 269–72 and 647. Cleon's family
evidently owned and ran a tannery, a distinctly odorous business and
jokes about reeking smells are common about Cleon in comedy. At 313
he is called 'Cerberus down there'. This is part of a running joke against
Cleon who, it seems, referred to himself as 'the watch-dog of the people'
(*Kn.* 1023–4) and for that reason was brought on stage in *Wasps* as
Cyon ('the dog'). On two other occasions he is mentioned as now

residing in the Underworld, 'eating shit in Hades' (47–9) and at 648–56 after Hermes has mentioned 'the leather-seller':

> TRYG: Stop, lord Hermes, stop, say no more. But leave that man exactly where he is, down there. That makes him no longer ours, but yours. So whatever you say about him, even if in life he was a villain and shot his mouth off, an informer and shit-disturber and trouble-maker, when you say all this, you are really insulting one of your own.

In the *parabasis* (752–9) Aristophanes repeats the brilliant passage from *Wasps* 1030–6 in which he portrays Cleon as a fearsome monster to be defeated by Aristophanes as Heracles:

> with the passion of a Heracles he would take on the very greatest of monsters, wading through the frightful reek of leather hides and the threats of an angry muck-raker. And first of all I fight against the Jag-Tooth himself, from whose eyes blazed most frightening rays of the Bitch-Star and in a circle around his head hissed the heads of a hundred damned sycophants. It had the voice of a destructive torrent in flood, the stink of a seal, the unwashed balls of a Lamia, and the arse-hole of a camel. Faced with such a terror he felt no fear.

This is the last that we hear in extant Aristophanes about Cleon, apart from a brief mention years later at *Frogs* 569–70, where a wronged baking-woman seeking redress from 'Heracles' (in fact a disguised Dionysus) summons the dead demagogues Cleon and Hyperbolus to her aid.

Hyperbolus was by trade a lamp-maker, which allows Trygaeus at *Peace* 679–92 to conclude humorously that having a lamp-maker as a leader will 'allow us to conduct enlightened deliberation'. He becomes a comic target in the early 420s and *Peace* 690, 'who now rules the rock on the Pnyx?' shows that in the public eye he had 'succeeded' to the unofficial position of *prostatēs tou dēmou* ('leader of the people'). Eupolis produced a demagogue-comedy about him called *Maricas* at the Lenaea of 421, 'disguising' Hyperbolus under the Persian name, 'Maricas', which had the connotations of youth, foreign birth, roguery and sexual perversion. As Eupolis would have begun work on this comedy before Cleon died at Amphipolis, Hyperbolus was prominent enough by late 422 to have been the target of an entire comedy.

Comedians accused Cleon and the other demagogues of resorting to inflammatory rhetoric in their public speeches and to have used prosecutions in the courts as a tactic to discredit and impede political rivals. In Athenian legal cases the person launching the prosecution would make the accusatory speeches in court. They are often called *rhētores*, meaning literally 'speakers' but possessing the modern connotation of 'politicians'. Trygaeus at *Peace* 632–43 uses the term *tous legontas* ('speakers') and presents the comic view of their activity during the war years:

> And here when the working people came in from the countryside, they did not realise that they were being sold out in the same way. In their lack of grape-pips and their desire for figs they kept looking to the speakers. These knew very well that the poor were growing weak and lacking for barley-grains and drove this goddess away with forked cries whenever she appeared with longing for this land. They would shake down those among the allies who were fat and rich, drumming up such charges as 'he is in league with Brasidas'. Then like puppy dogs you people would tear that man apart, for the city was hungry and cowering in fear, and devoured very gladly whatever slanders were served to it.

The question is again how serious is Aristophanes' depiction of Cleon and the other demagogues? Was he writing comedy or satire? A modern assumption, not restricted to undergraduate students, is that making fun of someone or something is meant to be intentionally hostile. Thus, Aristophanes and the other comic poets become conscious advocates of a 'right-wing agenda', their caricatures of Socrates reflect a conservative distaste for anything 'modern' and intellectual, and Aristophanes preferred the traditional tragedies of Aeschylus to the new and disturbing dramas of Euripides. But comedy is always attracted by what is strange and in vogue, and the demagogues were something new and different on the political scene. Their distinctive and flamboyant style would have been natural material for comedy and once the stereotype described above had been established, the comic poets could exploit it at will, whether or not there was much truth to their allegations.

In the case of Cleon, however, Aristophanes' hostility seems to be genuine and personal. They both came from the same deme (Cydathenaeon), and although this may indicate only where their grandfathers lived when Cleisthenes established the deme structure in 507, there could be personal local issues at work here. Added to any personal motives Cleon's political style would have offended traditionally minded Athenians. Comedy repeatedly pokes fun at his manner of public speaking, comparing his voice to the squeal of a scalded pig or a roaring river in flood. Politically he supported an aggressive war policy and is blamed for rejecting the Spartan peace proposals after Pylos. Since Aristophanes' early plays display a strong anti-war theme, at least anti-*this*-war, Cleon's pro-war stance could hardly have been acceptable to Aristophanes. Add to this his vulgar tactics in the assembly and exploitation in the law-courts and we may conclude that there is more than just humour involved in the caricature of Cleon. *Peace* gives Aristophanes the opportunity to prod the corpse of Cleon a few more times, just to be certain that he really is dead.

Aristophanes re-writes recent history

Following the chorus' enthusiastic welcome of Peace, we get an unusual scene (601–56) involving Hermes, Trygaeus and a silent figure of Peace. The metre is trochaic tetrameter catalectic, not rare in comedy, but most commonly found in the formal epirrhematic sections of a *parabasis* (as at *Peace* 1140–55, 1172–87) and in the entry scenes of the chorus, where it usually accompanies an excited exchange on stage between one or more of the characters and the chorus. There is nothing in extant Aristophanes like this explanatory scene in trochaics from *Peace*. Some observe the absence of a formal *agōn* in the play and pointing to the expositions in *Acharnians*, *Birds* and *Women at the Assembly* that replace the expected *agōn*, argue that this scene here serves the same function of the missing *agōn*. On another explanation these trochaics may be replacing the formal trochaic *epirrhemata* that are absent from the first *parabasis*. But neither explanation really fits what happens in this scene where the leader of the chorus asks Hermes why the goddess 'was away from us for such a long time' (601).

Hermes replies (605) that 'it all started when Pheidias got into trouble'. Pericles had put Pheidias in charge of the re-building of the Acropolis (Plutarch *Per.* 13) and attributed to him personally are the great statues of Athena Promachos on the Acropolis, the Athena Parthenos inside the Parthenon, and the statue of Zeus at Olympia, the last ranked by the ancients as one of the Seven Wonders of the World. Certain ancient sources report that when he was accused of appropriating some of the gold (or ivory) used in the statuary, rather than face the sentence of the law-courts at Athens he chose to flee to Olympia, where he then sculpted the statue of Zeus. Hermes goes on to say that Pericles, who was linked personally with Pheidias and also a member of the board supervising the work, feared that the scandal might spill over onto him. The ancient sources record a number of legal prosecutions in the 430s of Pericles' friends and associates, intended as indirect attacks on the leader himself. Accordingly, Pericles 'set the city on fire by throwing down a tiny spark of a Megarian decree' (608–9). The significance of this decree is discussed below.

Two problems arise here. First, the scholiast to *Peace* 606 declares the story 'untenable' (*alogos*), citing the third-century historian Philochorus (*FGrHist* 328 F 121), who confidently dates 'Pheidias' trouble' six years before the decree against the Megarians (432/1) although he does confuse the names of two year-archons.[7] More crucial, however, is the reaction of Trygaeus and the chorus to Hermes' narrative (615–8):

> TRYG: By Apollo, I have never been told this by anyone before nor had
>   I heard that Pheidias had anything to do with her [Peace].
> CHOR: Nor had I, until just now.

This should have suggested to any alert reader or spectator that this story connecting Pheidias, Pericles and the War was only a comic fabrication. But Diodorus of Sicily 12.39 included this story seriously in his account of Pericles' motivation to begin hostilities and the scholiast to *Peace* 606 adds that 'some say' that Pericles 'started the war . . . so that the Athenians would be too occupied with the war to pursue him in the courts.' Probably included among the 'some' would be the respected fourth-century historian Ephorus, one of Diodorus' major sources.[8] To preserve a reasonable historicity some modern scholars have proposed downdating the accusations against Pheidias to around 434 or 433, to create a more natural segué to the Megarian decrees, but the whole point of this narrative is that Pheidias' trouble has nothing to do with the outbreak of war and that this connection is an invention by a comic poet. Since Trygaeus' reference to Pheidias' misbehaviour suggests that this was not something new to the spectators in 421, there may well have been accusations of misconduct against Pericles and his friends, but Podlecki (1988: 109) would argue that these were not formal legal actions against the friends of Pericles, but similar comic inventions by poets in the 430s, perhaps influenced by or influencing public gossip.

This is also not the only instance where something in Old Comedy was taken to be sober fact and so reported by later writers. For example, in the seventh hypothesis to *Clouds* we read that the accusers of Socrates suborned Aristophanes to attack Socrates in *Clouds* as part of their campaign against him, despite the fact that twenty-three years elapsed between the production of *Clouds* (Dionysia of 423) and the legal action against Socrates in 399. Nor is this the only instance in *Peace* where exact chronology is amiss: the implication at 700–3 that Cratinus died 'when the Spartans invaded' (431) when he was active as late as 423, and Trygaeus' lament at 990 that 'we have missed you for thirteen years', when Thucydides (5.20.1) states that the first part of the war had lasted for 'ten years and a few days'.

There are similar elements in Dicaeopolis' account of the cause of the war at *Ach.* 514–56. He blames the war first of all on trouble-making informers who were over-enthusiastic in their actions against trade-goods from the neighbouring city of Megara. This was supposedly followed by the abduction by some young Athenians of a Megarian prostitute (*pornē*) named Simaithe and the Megarians' response of 'stealing two of Aspasia's whores' (527). Dicaeopolis continues:

> And so the war broke out over all of Greece as a result of three harlots. Then Olympian Pericles in his wrath thundered and lightened and stirred up all of Greece, proposing decrees sounding like drinking-songs that 'no Megarians should remain on the earth or in the market-place, on the sea or on the mainland'. Then the Megarians, who were gradually starving to death, begged the Spartans to get that decree of the three harlots overturned.

Both this account and that in *Peace* consider the Megarian decree as the crucial *casus belli*, whereas Thucydides (1.65–7) downplays the action against Megara, preferring to concentrate on the larger conflicts between Athens and the Spartan allies elsewhere. Both comic accounts show Pericles acting from personal motives connected with someone close to him, his mistress Aspasia (called a *pornē* at Eupolis F 110) and his associate Pheidias. The scholiast to *Ach.* 525 assumes that the theft of Simathe was a real event and identified one of the Athenian young men as Alcibiades who had fallen in lust with her, yet another example of comedy being taken as fact. It is significant that Aristophanes more than seven years after Pericles' death still harbours a definite hostility against him for his responsibility for the Archidamian War.

Peace and peace

Aristophanes would have been working on *Peace* during the peace negotiations that took place in the early months of 421 and resulted in the signing of a treaty between the Spartans and Athenians 'immediately after the City Dionysia' of 421 (Thuc. 5.20). We know that the archon eponymous,[9] the official in charge of the conduct of the City Dionysia, began his duties soon after assuming office in early July by assigning *chorēgoi* for the competitions in comedy and tragedy. We do not know how early in his year of office he would select the actual comic poets who would compete, but early September would allow seven months for rehearsal for the Dionysia. Hostilities after the year of truce in 423/2 did not resume 'until the Pythian games' (Thuc. 5.1), celebrated in August or early September of 422, and thus the battle at Amphipolis was likely not fought until mid-October.[10] Thus, Aristophanes would have already decided on a comedy about achieving peace before the deaths of Cleon and Brasidas made the serious negotiations possible. Thucydides makes it clear that the truce of 423/2 enjoyed popular support and that the resumption of the fighting, two months after the truce officially ended, was instigated by Cleon (Thuc. 5.2) to deal with unresolved issues in the North. We can only speculate how different the comic idea that Aristophanes pitched to the archon was from the play that he actually performed at the Dionysia, but it seems likely that Trygaeus' mission on the dung-beetle was part of the original proposal. The plot changes when Hermes informs Trygaeus that War has taken over Olympus and locked Peace up in a cave. At that point the great idea shifts to the physical rescue of Peace. As a peace treaty was becoming more and more likely during the early months of 421, the poet may have preferred to celebrate the imminent treaty rather than even raise any serious opposition to Trygaeus' plan. In the other two 'peace plays' (*Acharnians, Lysistrata*), peace is not an immediate prospect but a fantastic dream. Thus, an actual opponent (the hostile Acharnians and Lamachus, the old men and the *proboulos*) makes for effective drama.[11]

In the early months of 421 how confident were the Athenians that the current negotiations would be successful? Opinions range from those of Murray (1933: 61), 'the cause ... was already won', and de Ste Croix (1972: 368), 'peace was certainly coming soon', to the more cautious view of Sommerstein (1985: xvi), 'now within the grasp of the Greek people, *if* they will make one final effort', to the pessimistic conclusions of Sicking (1967: 116), 'in the first months of the year 421 a common peace of any sort was not really to be expected',[12] and Tordoff (2011: 198 n.71), 'negotiations that might easily have collapsed'. We might read the comedy in three ways: a fond dream that *was* now coming true – the most common view of the play, a fond dream that

might come true, or a fond dream that couldn't come true. On the last
reading the play becomes a wonderful and delightful fantasy about an
idyllic pastoral existence, but with the benefit of hindsight we might
agree with Kagan (1974: 349), 'though the Athenians were able to drag
peace onto the scene in 421, her visit was not likely to be long'.

In *Acharnians* and *Lysistrata* peace is achieved through negotiation
between Athenians and Spartans, but here through the fanciful rescue
of a goddess from a cave, in a setting that is out of this world. The failed
negotiations in the past are mentioned in the comedy (211–20, 663–7),
but not the current talks. In the rescue-scene certain contemporary
events may be glimpsed. Hermes and Trygaeus single out the
uncooperative Boeotians and Megarians (464–6, 500–2), both of whom
would oppose the eventual peace accord between Athens and Spartan
(Thuc. 5.17.2), while the Argives are accused of tugging in both
directions (475–7). Other references in comedy confirm that the
Argives were playing a double game in the late 420s (*Kn.* 465–6,
Pherecrates F 22, 'these damned people are sitting in our way and
playing both sides against the middle'). Thucydides (5.27–31) reveals
how immediately after the signing of the treaty the Argives began
building an alliance and 'reaped a harvest' of disaffected states without
having fought in the previous hostilities. At 473–4 the Athenian general
Lamachus is imagined as impeding the rescue of Peace, 'it's not right for
you to get in the way, we certainly don't need your bogey'. This may just
be a continuation of the joke that Lamachus had on his shield the image
of a Gorgon which the comedian turns into a 'bogey' (*mormō*) (*Ach.*
567, 574, 582 etc.), but Lamachus was one of signatories to the peace
accord (5.19) and this could hint at his less than enthusiastic support.

Ach. 501–6 shows that foreign visitors attended the City Dionysia. If
envoys from Sparta or from any other Greek states involved in the war
were actually present in the theatre, how might they have reacted to
what was said in the comedy? While Hermes casts both Spartans and
Athenians in an unflattering light at 210–22, Trygaeus does admit at
477 that 'the Spartans *are* pulling strongly'. Hermes, however, is quick to
point out that these are the Spartan prisoners from Pylos and they just

want to get free. At 625–7 Hermes observes that, as at Athens, it was the Spartan farmer who suffered the most from enemy raids, but later adds that Spartan leaders could be easily bribed.[13] Since recovering those captured at Pylos was a major impetus behind Sparta's desire for a peace, Aristophanes could be gently suggesting to any Spartans present that should the negotiations fail, the prisoners will remain at Athens, and to the Athenians that surrendering the prisoners is essential to a successful peace. Slater (2002: 124) proposed that when Hermes notices at 538–40 that 'the cities now reconciled are happily chatting and laughing with one another', he could be pointing out these foreign visitors at the theatre. However, at this point Hermes seems to be speaking generally about Greece and only turns his attention to the theatre at line 543.

To sum up, Aristophanes would have probably presented his proposal for a comedy at the Dionysia of 421 during the summer of 422 and certainly before the deaths of Cleon and Brasidas, the 'pestles of War', at Amphipolis allowed serious peace negotiations to begin. But as the pace of talks accelerated and the prospect of a successful conclusion became more and more likely, the poet abandoned any direct dramatic confrontation with an opponent to peace, and decided to celebrate the restoration of Peace, her installation as a presiding goddess, and the return to an idyllic life in the country.

Themes and Motifs in *Peace*

The previous chapter considered how we might read *Peace* against the background of the actual treaty that was being negotiated in the early months of 421: confident celebration or wistful dream. In this chapter I want to examine certain repeated and larger themes in *Peace*, such as the folk-tale themes of monsters, divine beings and the quest. Of the eleven extant plays, *Peace* is perhaps the one most concerned with divine settings and characters. Then there are the recurring motifs of aromas, food and sex, the attractive ones that come with Peace and the unpleasant ones that belong to wartime. Other Aristophanic comedies play with the opposition between town and country, but the theme of 'back to the country' could be this comedy's sub-title. Why was a statue used for the rescued goddess and not a mute actor as in other comedies? Trygaeus claims to be acting for all the Greeks (Panhellenes), but is not the comedy more about Athens? Finally, of all the surviving plays *Peace* most breaks down the boundary between players and spectators, and co-opts the latter into the dramatic action. Some final thoughts will address the exuberant fantasy of 'back to the country . . . and to the past'. There is much here both to intrigue and delight the interested reader.

The monsters in *Peace*

Alongside the ordered world of the Olympian gods, the Greek mythical tradition possessed what we would call 'monsters', who find their way into the genres of Greek drama. Tragedy for the most part avoids such creatures, although we do see a chorus of monstrous Furies in Aeschylus' *Eumenides* (458) and the ancient deity Lyssa ('Madness') at *Heracles*

822, perhaps winged and holding snakes. Monsters are mentioned in tragedy but they tend not to appear. F 145 of *Andromeda* suggests that Perseus' rescue of the princess from the sea-monster was handled in a messenger-speech, like that relating Hippolytus' encounter with the bull (1173–1254). But both satyr-drama and comedy featured terrifying and powerful creatures whom the principal character must confront and overcome. As early as Epicharmus (510–470) we find comedies with titles that suggest an encounter between human hero and monster: *Busiris, Pholus, Sphinx, Cyclops* and *Sciron.* Four of these titles recur in later Athenian comedy or satyr-drama. Sommerstein (1998: 20) sums up the essentials of a comic monster: 'fearsome appearance, fearsome sound-effects, tendency to eat people, eventual defeat by a hero'.

In Athenian Old Comedy several plays by Cratinus belonged to this tradition. In the 430s both his *Odysseus and Company* and Callias' *Cyclopes* dramatized the story of Odysseus' encounter with the Cyclops in *Odyssey* 9. Cratinus also wrote a *Busiris* and his *All-Seers* seems to have had multiple examples of Argos, the many-eyed creature that guarded Io. *Chirons* presumably had a chorus of these man-horse beings, and in his *Runaways,* Theseus recounts his slaying of Cercyon (F 53). Crates, a comic poet of the 430s, wrote a comedy named for Lamia, a grotesque creature of myth, who is part of Aristophanes' depiction of Cleon in *Wasps* and *Peace.* Also mentioned are such bogey-women as Mormo (*Peace* 474, F 31) and the Empousa (*Frogs* 280–95).

Aristophanes and Eupolis avoided mythological burlesques with plots and characters set in the world of myth (e.g., Cratinus' *Dionysalexander* and *Nemesis*) and preferred to focus on the people and issues of the contemporary city. Gods do become involved in the events of the play, but in Aristophanes they come to our world, although Trygaeus' brief visit to Olympus in *Peace* is an obvious exception. Sommerstein (1998) has shown that Aristophanes prefers human antagonists with monstrous attributes for the comic hero to overcome. Lamachus in *Acharnians* is summoned by the chorus to their aid and enters menacingly bearing a shield emblazoned with a Gorgon and wearing a triple-crested helmet. But by the end of the play he is carried off half-dead while Dicaeopolis leaves in triumph in the arms of dancing-girls. By the end of *Knights* Paphlagon (Cleon), who 'doth bestride the narrow world like a Colossus' (74-9), is sent to peddle sausages at the city gates while his adversary, the Sausage-Seller, retires to enjoy a free dinner at the Prytaneion. *Wasps* opens with a description of Cleon as 'an all-devouring sea-monster with the voice of a scalded sow' (35-6).

In *Peace* there are two monsters, one off-stage and the other a speaking character. First there is Cleon, now dead and called 'Cerberus down there' (313-15). Trygaeus worries that 'by his shouting and screaming he might get in the way of our dragging the goddess out.' Later (648-9), Aristophanes insists the best course is to leave him 'down there' and not mention him any further. Then in the *parabasis* proper of *Peace* (752-9) he repeats his brilliant description of the Cleon-monster from *Wasps*, turning himself into a Heracles, famous in Greek myth for challenging and slaying monsters. The poet is now the hero of his own personal drama, wading through reeking leather hides and braving the threats of the Jag-tooth himself.

The second monster is War whose appearance is forecast by Hermes. The text gives no real details about his appearance, apart from a fearsome look in his eyes (239), but he might well have been costumed like Lamachus in *Acharnians* (565-625,1071-1143).[1] There is a terrible noise in the background, but it is the sound of the mortar from inside the house (233-5). His bluster reminds one of the giant in *Jack and the Beanstalk*, and he behaves with menacing authority to his underling Riot. But when he cannot acquire the pestle needed to pound up the various Greek cities into a savoury-mash, he retires from the scene and is not heard from again. When Hermes tries to thwart their attempt to rescue Peace (361-425), it is not War he calls to, but Zeus. There are monsters in this comedy, but one is dead and not to be disturbed and the other vanishes with no threat to the continuing plot-line. Unlike other comic heroes who confront a monstrous antagonist and bring the play's great ideal to fulfilment, the only obstacle to realizing Trygaeus' great idea is the Greeks' own lack of enthusiasm.

Gods and other divine beings in *Peace*

Greek gods were no strangers to Athenian drama. Gods appear in all three genres, tragedy and comedy and satyr-drama, often for an opening or closing scene, on occasion dominating an entire drama (*Prometheus Bound*). As speaking characters in Aristophanes we meet Hermes (*Peace, Wealth*), Poseidon (*Birds*), Heracles (*Birds, Frogs*), Dionysus (*Frogs*), Plouton (*Frogs*), Iris (*Birds*), Ploutos (*Wealth*) and a chorus of Clouds called 'awesome goddesses' (*Cl.* 265).[2] Cratinus had choruses of Wealth-Gods and Chirons, Hermes and three goddesses appeared in his *Dionysalexander*, and his *Nemesis*, describing the birth of Helen, must also have had divine characters among its cast. Several titles of Hermippus' comedies, an earlier contemporary of Aristophanes, had gods in major roles: *Birth of Athena, Gods, Fates*. The comic poet Platon wrote a *Zeus Badly Treated*, in which Heracles was a character. Comic deities can include the traditional Olympians, and also personified concepts, as in our play War and Riot, Holiday and Harvest.

When Trygaeus reaches Olympus, he discovers from Hermes, in a familiar role as Olympian errand-boy, that he will not be able to confront Zeus as he had intended, since 'the gods moved out yesterday ... to under the very dome of heaven' (197–9). The gods have handed Olympus over to War, who can do with the Greeks what he likes, while they 'moved house as high as they could so that they wouldn't see you fighting any more and have to listen to your pleadings' (207–9). The Titans may have been displaced by the Olympians and removed to the depths of Tartarus, but a voluntary and mass exodus of the gods does not seem to have been part of Greek myth, although Bowie (1993: 142–3) does suggest some ritual parallels for the withdrawal and return of a displeased or displaced divinity.

The gods have left Greeks in the hands of War, who is a personification rather than an actual deity. The earlier fifth-century poet Pindar (F 78.1) had called War-Cry as 'daughter of War' and in Aristophanes' comedy of 425 *Acharnians* the chorus at 971–85 imagine War as a violent and unwelcome guest at a symposium: 'he was a violent drunk

... and caused all sorts of harm ... he set even more of vine stakes on fire and forcibly squeezed all the wine from our vines.' Aristophanes gives him the role of the monstrous antagonist in our comedy, but as we have seen, the comic plot does not proceed along the lines of tricking or defeating the monster to fulfil the quest. The imagery of the drinking party from *Acharnians* is replaced by that of preparing food, specifically a savoury-mash with leeks from Prasiae, honey from Attica, garlic from Megara and cheese from Sicily. Each of these cities is imagined as being added to the mortar to be crushed by a pestle. Unfortunately for War there is no pestle on Olympus and both Athens and Sparta have lost theirs, the war-leaders Cleon and Brasidas. War is no longer the guest at a party, he is now the cook.

Hermes is one of comedy's favourite gods, partly because of his many epithets and roles – a short scene at the end of *Wealth* turns on Hermes' finding which of his many talents will give him a place in the new regime. He is finally allowed in as Hermes Diakonikos ('errand boy'). In *Peace*, he is at first the hostile door-keeper, a familiar figure in comedy, since knocking at a strange door is always good comic material. When he threatens Trygaeus, he is easily distracted by the offer of a good cut of meat (192–4, 378–9) and is bribed not to say anything to Zeus about Trygaeus' scheme to rescue Peace – 'I really have been rather fond of gold' (425). Hermes is more humorous than sinister and takes the role of Trygaeus' straight-man.

Some have read into the departure of Zeus and the other Olympian gods a sign of contemporary disaffection with the gods. If we had more of Euripides' lost *Bellerophon*, we might know how strongly the gods were criticized in that tragedy. A character at F 286, probably not Bellerophon, flatly denies that there are gods in heaven and attributes belief in them to human folly. The scene between Hermes and Trygaeus (196–222) shows that the gods are not to blame for the war, but rather humans themselves, and that their entreaties have annoyed the gods so much that they have left humanity to its own devices. Trygaeus admits at 220 that 'those words are our very stamp'. Zeus has placed a penalty of doom on anyone who dared rescue Peace (361–80) and there is a

moment of potential disaster when Hermes begins to summon him
(376). But Hermes is easily distracted by the offer of gold and the
revelation of an unlikely conspiracy of the Moon and the Sun against
the Olympians (382–425). Peace is not installed as a goddess to replace
the Olympians, although it is not clear whether the Olympians will
return once Peace has returned. In *Birds*, Peisetaerus arrives at the end
(1706–65) in triumph with Princess, Zeus' daughter, as his bride and
wielding the divine thunderbolt, and at the end of *Wealth* (1171–1208)
the once-blind god is about to be installed formally and the priest of
Zeus Saviour, now out of a job, arrives to join the new regime only to
discover that Zeus Saviour has already come over to the winning side.
In our comedy, Peace is elevated to a formal divine status with all the
benefits which she will bring to humanity, especially to the farmers of
Greece. Olson (1998: xli) makes the good point that 'what matters in
Peace is thus not theology but politics'.

The fairy-tale world of *Peace*

Most of the Greek myths we know have to do with the Olympian gods
and their relationship with the mortal world. In the Homeric epics the
major divine players are part of the Olympian theocracy, and even
minor figures such as Thetis and Iris are well worked into the traditional
pantheon. Likewise, in fifth-century tragedy, the gods who influence
and appear in the action are for the most part the familiar Olympians,
and minor figures such as Lyssa (Madness, in Euripides' *Heracles*) or
Kratos (Power, in *Prometheus Bound*) are partnered with traditional
figures such as Iris and Hephaestus. Satyr-drama often ventured into
the realm of the magical and the monstrous. Euripides' *Cyclops* comically
dramatized the encounter of Odysseus and the man-eating Cyclops in
Odyssey 9, Sophocles' lost *Trackers* presented the infancy of Hermes, the
trickster god who steals his brother's cattle on the day after he was born,
and Euripides' *Autolycus* the greatest thief in antiquity who possessed
quasi-magical powers to aid his thefts. Especially revealing is Euripides'

Alcestis, produced in 438 in the fourth position usually occupied by a satyr-drama. But there are no satyrs in *Alcestis*, and the critics disagree whether the play should be considered tragedy, tragicomedy or a satyr-drama in disguise. But the divine universe is not that of the traditional Olympians. Zeus can compel Apollo to serve a mortal (Admetus) for a year, Apollo can grant Admetus the power to avoid death if he can find someone else to die in his place, and Heracles can wrestle with Death to win back the dead Alcestis. Death in *Alcestis* is not Hades or Plouton, but Thanatos who, like the Grim Reaper, arrives with blade in hand to claim Alcestis.

This is the folk-culture of the ancient Greeks. The fables of Aesop, traditionally sixth-century, have talking animals, a simply told tale and an obvious moral. The flight of Trygaeus to Olympus on the gigantic dung-beetle is expressly related to the fable by Aesop about the eagle and the beetle (127–30):

> GIRL: And what is your purpose, father, that you have harnessed a
> beetle and are riding to the gods?
> TRYG: It's recorded in the tales of Aesop that it is the only winged
> creature to have reached the gods.

The various versions of the tale agree that the beetle was constantly destroying the nest and the eggs of an eagle until the eagle fled to the throne of Zeus as a safe place to lay her eggs. The beetle then flew up and distracted Zeus with the result that he dislodged and destroyed the eagle's eggs. Thus, the opening scenes are a mixture of the folk-tale motif of the beetle that could fly to the gods and a parody of the ascent of Bellerophon upon Pegasus in Euripides' lost tragedy of that name.

War belongs to this world of monsters, in good company with the Cyclops of *Odyssey* 9, adversaries of Heracles such as Geryon or Busiris, or those in the tales about Theseus (Sciron, Procrustes, even the Minotaur). War could have been the dramatic antagonist for Trygaeus, to be overcome for the great idea to succeed. We do have such a scene at *Ach.* 572–625, where Lamachus enters menacingly to confront Dicaeopolis who has dared make peace with the Spartans. But Aristophanes shifts the plot to another folk-tale motif, the physical rescue of an imprisoned female. Olson (1998: xxxvi–xxxviii) finds certain folk-tale themes that bear upon the rescue of Peace. In the first, 'a god or (more often) a goddess emerges from the earth, bringing with him or her renewed agricultural fertility'. This is best known from the *Homeric Hymn to Demeter* (*c.* 600), in which Demeter's daughter, abducted by her uncle Hades to be his bride, now resides in the Underworld. Demeter in despair removes fertility from the earth and relents only when Zeus dispatches Hermes to return Persephone to the upper world. Parallels with *Peace* would be the agency of Hermes, who may not take an active part in the drawing out of Peace but who does superintend the action, the return of a beautiful goddess from a captivity, and the resulting benefits for the growth of crops (especially grapes and figs).

Olson (1998: xxxvi–xxxvii) calls our attention to a number of fifth-century vases which may bear upon the emergence of Peace from her underground captivity. First is a splendid bell-*kratēr* in New York, by the Persephone Painter and dated to the 440s. Hermes is escorting Persephone up out of the earth, while Hecate walks ahead holding torches to lead the maiden back to her mother Demeter. Next is a volute-*kratēr* in Oxford, dated *c.* 440, depicting Pandora emerging from the ground with Epimetheus standing beside her holding a mallet (*sphyra*) while Zeus and Hermes look on. Finally, in Ferrara is a fine *kratēr*, dated *c.* 445, which shows satyrs holding *sphyrai* and dancing about a female figure only partially emerged from beneath the earth. A male figure stands behind her holding either unlit torches or staves.[3] At *Peace* 566–7 a *sphyra* is one of the implements used in the rescue of Peace. Olson concludes reasonably that 'a story-pattern in which a god or goddess emerged from the earth or the Underworld (sometimes represented specifically by a cave) under the escort of Hermes in order to restore fertility to the world was relatively widespread in Greece in the classical period and would have been recognized by Aristophanes' audience when he put it to use in *Peace*'.

Olson relates *Peace* to two other folk-tale motifs, the 'Raid on the Ogre's Lair' and the 'Rescue of the Woman in Distress'. Examples of the first would be Odysseus and the Cyclops in *Odyssey* 9, Jason and the Golden Fleece, and in recent times Bilbo and the dragon Smaug. Repeated motifs include the journey to a distant locale, overcoming the monster, and returning with treasure. In *Peace*, the journey is to Olympus, the monster is War, and the treasure is Peace and all the blessings that she brings (530–7, 571–81, 987–1005, 1127–90). The tale of the 'damsel in distress' has become a mainstay of adventure stories of all sorts. In classical myth we may cite Jason and Medea, Perseus and Andromeda, Orestes and Iphigeneia – it was especially popular in Euripides' 'romantic tragedies' such as *Helen*, *Andromeda*, etc. The hero usually journeys to a distant land, defeats or tricks a monstrous figure who holds the damsel prisoner, and returns home to marry his newfound love. In Aristophanes' comedy it is not the goddess Peace whom the hero weds at the end, but her handmaiden Harvest.

Peace and the countryside

Aristophanes belonged to the city deme of Cydathenaeon, a prosperous area north-east of the Acropolis. But *Peace* is a hymn to the delights of country life before the war. In the prologue of *Acharnians*, Dicaeopolis, a countryman from the deme Cholleidai, longs for his deme and wants only to go home. At 201–2 he is ostensibly back in his deme to celebrate the Rural Dionysia, but by 729 the scene is again Athens and the characters and background of the second half of the play belong more properly to the city. In *Knights*, Cleon and the other supporters of war have forced Demos ('The People') 'to live in barrels and back alleys and attics' (792–3), while they continue to profit personally from the conflict. 'But if he ever goes back to the country [*eis agron*] and lives in a time of peace, regaining his courage from eating grits and having close contact with pressed olives, then he will discover what good things you have cheated him out of with your welfare payments' (805–7).

The prologue and early scenes of *Peace* do not mention either the farmers or the countryside. Farmers are certainly the first to be summoned at 296–8, but immediately after come 'merchants and carpenters, craftsmen and metics, foreigners and islanders'. It is not until the hauling-scene (508–11) that the farmers become the prime players, and from that point on the countryside takes over the play. Peace is hailed as 'giver of grapes' (520), her attendants are named as Harvest and Holiday, and Holiday's scent is a delightful mixture of aromas from the countryside and the springtime festival (530–8). The phrase *eis agron* ('to the country') becomes a recurring refrain in this play. Half of the uses of *agros* in extant Aristophanes come from *Peace*, especially from the scene that welcomes the goddess (520–600). Hermes mentions (612–14) that the first casualties of war were the grapevine and the wine-jar, that the Athenian warships wrought similar havoc on the Spartan farmers (625–7), and that, as in *Knights*, the rural population was being forced into an unfamiliar and hostile urban environment (632–5).

The second *parabasis* (1127–90) has been justly praised for its compelling fantasy of an ideal life in the country in a time of peace. In the ode and *epirrhēma*, the chorus present a dramatic dialogue between two neighbours planning a pleasant afternoon in winter-time while the gentle rains pour down: 'there is nothing more pleasant than to have the sowing done, for the god to pour down rain gently, and for a neighbour to enquire, "Tell me, Comarchides,[4] what shall we do today"?' The antode (1159–71) moves to the summer, 'when the cicada chirps his sweet song' and the speaker inspects his early-blooming vines and swelling figs, 'and then I get fat at that time of the summer.'

The *antepirrhēma* (1172–90) moves abruptly from a time of peace in the country to the city and the vision of a 'god-hated trierarch with three crests and a purple cloak' who is the first to flee the line of battle and alters the military call-up lists at his convenience and of a man from the Pandion tribe who discovers that next day he must leave on active service. 'That's the way they treat us country-folk [*tous agroikous*], but not so much those from the city'. Since the tribe mentioned at 1183 is Pandion, Aristophanes' own tribe, a personal experience may lurk beneath the chorus' complaint. While the military might of Athens lay more with its navy rather than its land forces, the emphasis throughout the play is on the hardships of serving on land, 'with spear, with shield' (356), Peace 'who hates shield-bands the most' (662), and the weapons offered by the arms-dealer (1210–64). As the encounter imagined in these lines is clearly a land-battle, Olson (1998: 292) wonders if there is not one last shot at Cleon, whom Thucydides accuses of turning to run away well before the rest of his army at Amphipolis (5.10.9).

In this comedy there is a definite antithesis between country (*agron*) and city (*asty*). The latter is a place for 'fierce and bad-tempered jurymen' (349), where soldiers train for war (356), where the politicians exploit the poor and the assembly is persuaded to reject peace (635–7, 665–7), where Hyperbolus the lamp-maker 'now rules the rock' (680), where Hierocles the bogus oracle-monger chants his false prophecies, and where the taxiarchs meddle with the call-up lists to the detriment of the country-people (1179–90). The city is a place of contention, exploitation, verbal deception and military discipline as opposed to the pastoral depiction of country-life, where Peace creates a harmony between humans and nature (584–600) and where an unselfish and mutual co-operation is the norm (1127–58). The Athenian agora will be filled with good produce from currently hostile states, 'from Megara garlic, early cucumbers, apples and pomegranates, little woollen cloaks; from Boeotia geese and ducks, pigeons and wrens, and baskets of Copaic eels. Among these goods may we all do our shopping together' (999–1007).

So, is Aristophanes then essentially a lover of the country, uncomfortable in the hustle and bustle of the city? His characters often seek to be 'free from *pragmatōn* (problems)' and these *pragmata* seem to be associated to living in a city. Dicaeopolis wants to return to his deme, while Peisetaerus and Euelpides in *Birds* flee their city for a 'comfortable (*apragmona*) spot'. But plays like *Knights* and *Wasps* and *Lysistrata* are so clearly based in the city and his chief characters so often involved in a mission 'to save the city', to use Dionysus' words at *Frogs* 1419, that we cannot consider Aristophanes as uncaring about his city and its institutions. On three occasions he can parody the procedure of the Athenian assembly, in *Knights* a meeting of the Council (624–82), and in *Wasps* the law-courts are transferred to Philocleon's house with all the paraphernalia thereof provided, but in comic fashion. Writing and producing comedies, sometimes two in a year, must have kept him in the city for months on end. If it were common for well-off city-dwellers to have a country property as well, this might explain his praise of the rural life, in the same way that modern urbanites extol that peaceful cottage by the lake.

At the end of *Knights* Demos ('The People') is restored to a life of 'the good old days', *Lysistrata* ends with a recalling of the golden age of Spartan-Athenian unity during the Persian Wars, *Frogs* with the resurrection of Aeschylus, again symbolic of an age of past glory. Rather than see Aristophanes as an unabashed lover of the country-side, the rural ideal presented in *Peace* could be one more of his nostalgic dreams. Such ideals were not unusual in Old Comedy. Athenaeus (267e–270a) lists seven comedies where the poets present a utopian (and unreal) existence as the substance of their dramas, often in terms of the easy availability of delicious foods.[5] Are the paeans to Peace and the countryside at 520–600, 974–1038, and 1127–90 the creations of a city dweller imagining an ideal life in the country? In a much later poem by the Roman poet Horace (late first century BCE), an idyllic musing on the pastoral life turns out to be thoughts of an urban moneylender about to start his daily routine (*Epode* 2). It is fair to say that for Aristophanes the country means a life of pleasure and co-operation and the city war and contentious behaviour.

Why a statue of Peace?

The scholiast to Plato *Apology* 19c records that both Eupolis (F 62 in his *Autolycus*, which we can date to 420) and Platon (F 86 in his *Victories*, probably early 410s) made fun of Aristophanes 'because he had set up the *kolossikon* of Peace'. It is not clear whether the point of the jokes was the size of the statue, the use of a statue instead of a mute female character, or a malfunction of the staging. The English sense of 'colossal' may mislead us into thinking that Aristophanes had brought a very large statue on stage, since the word in classical Greek, principally in Aeschylus and Herodotus, seems to have meant only a statue made of wood or wax or stone. It was the giant statue of Helios on Rhodes in the Hellenistic period that added the sense of hugeness to the word. When Herodotus (2.173–176) wants to emphasize the size of a statue, he either says *megalous kolossous* ('large statues') or gives the actual length or height. It is unlikely that the size of the statue was the source of the comic jokes.

Elsewhere, Aristophanes brings on silent actors to represent certain divine concepts or entities, usually female. We have the Truces (*Spondai*) at *Kn.* 1388–94, Princess (*Basileia*) in *Birds*, Reconciliation (*Diallagē*) in *Lysistrata* or the muse of Euripides in *Frogs*, as well as Peace's handmaidens, Holiday and Harvest. Very often these female figures are scantily dressed and introduced for the titillation of the male spectators. This is especially true of Reconciliation and Holiday, who are subjected to a series of verbal innuendoes and suggestive physical contact, the latter at *Peace* 868–915. By not having Peace played by a live actor, Aristophanes can avoid the sexual misbehaviour that we get elsewhere.

Trygaeus returns from Olympus with three divine women in tow, each with a different role and destiny in the drama. *Theōria* in Greek means 'watching' or 'spectating' and refers to going abroad to watch spectacles such as games or religious observances. 'Holiday' perhaps comes close to the idea of something to look forward to and which the War has made impossible. The first article of the treaty about to be signed was that anyone who so wished could travel freely and observe (*theōrein*) the common Greek celebrations without fear (Thuc. 5.18). Holiday is handed over to the *boulē*, the council with 500 members; her role is thus that of the woman of pleasure and the scene where she is handed over is full of not so subtle sexual innuendoes. Harvest, however, is to be the wife of Trygaeus: 'so then on those terms, receive Harvest to be your wife, live with her in the country [*en tois agrois*], and produce for yourself . . . grapes' (706–8). A formal wedding ceremony is to be prepared (842–5), and at the end of the comedy the traditional marriage procession is begun, which will mark also the ceremonial return to the country (*eis ton agron*). Finally, there is the figure of Peace, austere and motionless and silent, presiding over the scene before her.[6] To have had her speak would be to invest her with a personality, whereas Aristophanes wanted an august and symbolic figure here. Not all take a positive interpretation of Aristophanes' use of a statue. Sulprizio (2013: 54, 60) argues that it represents 'an idealised representation of traditional femininity: inert, enclosed ... and still susceptible to exploitative treatment' and that the treaty being established in 421 was 'like the statue that represented it on stage, it was peace in appearance only, weak and ineffective'.

In early Greek myth Peace was one of the daughters of Zeus and Themis known as the Horae ('Seasons'), along with Justice (*Dikē*) and Order (*Eunomia*), and was described by Hesiod (*Theogony* 902) as *tethalyia* ('blooming'). At his *Works and Days* 228 she is a personified concept, associated with Oath and Justice, who cares for those who keep honest judgements and do not forsake what is right: 'their city flourishes and the inhabitants blossom within it, for Peace the nurse of young men [*kourotrophos*] is on the earth'. But a formal cult of Peace was not established until the late 370s, following an Athenian victory over the Spartans in 375/4 and a subsequent peace in 371 (Isocrates 15.109–10), which would be celebrated every year with feasts and sacrifices. Plutarch (*Cimon* 13.6) dates the building of an altar to Peace in the aftermath of Cimon's great victory over the Persians at Eurymedon in the 460s, but he has very likely confused matters with the establishment in the 370s that Isocrates describes.

Even though there may have been no formal cult of Peace, the fifth-century poets and dramatists do invoke Peace as a personified entity. The elegist Theognis (late sixth century) links Peace and Wealth in his prayer, 'may Peace and Wealth possess my city, so that I may revel with others. I have no love for evil War' (885–6). The lyric poet Bacchylides (first half of the fifth century) contrasted life in peacetime with that in time of war in a passage that begins, 'Peace gives birth to great-hearted wealth for mortals' (*Paean* 4.61–80). The best-known dramatic example occurs at Euripides F 453, from his lost *Cresphontes* where the chorus of old men pray:

> Peace, deep in wealth and fairest of the gods, I yearn for you because you are so long in coming. I am afraid that old age may overwhelm me with troubles before I can behold your grace and beauty, the songs accompanied by dancing, and revellers wearing garlands. Come, lady [*potnia*], to our city and keep away from our homes hateful Unrest [*Stasis*] and furious Strife [*Eris*] whose joy is sharpened steel.

This ode was parodied in Aristophanes' *Farmers* (F 111), 'Peace, deep in wealth, and little yoke of oxen, I wish that I could have an end to war, to dig and trim vines, after a bath to munch white bread and cabbage, and to drain down a draught of new wine.' At *Suppliant Women* 489–91, a Theban herald argues that 'Peace is most dear to the Muses and the enemy of the Vengeful Spirits, she delights in the abundance of children and rejoices in wealth.' All three dramatic passages probably belong to the 420s.

In *Peace*, much is made of the association of Peace with the fruits of the earth, especially with grapes and wine. Trygaeus' name is related both to *trygan* ('harvest') and to *tryx* ('new wine'). The first of the formal invocations to the goddess begins with the words, 'Peace, bestower of grape-bunches, how should I address you? Where would I find a million-gallon name to call you by?' (520–2). Stafford (2000: 188) cites three representations of Peace on late fifth-century vases, all associated with Dionysus, the god of grapes and wine. On one a youthful Dionysus sits formally in the centre of the scene. Behind him reclines Peace holding a torch under one arm and a drinking horn in the other, and beside Dionysus is an attendant labelled 'Opora'.[7] Finally, Peace is personified in three poetic texts from the end of the fifth century. First at Euripides' *Orestes* 1682–3, Apollo dismisses Orestes and the other characters with the words, 'go now on your way, honouring Peace the fairest of the goddesses'. Then in *Bacchae*, Teiresias asserts that Dionysus 'loves Peace, giver of prosperity, child-nursing goddess' (419–20). Finally, F 15.240 of Timotheus has someone pray to Apollo, 'far-shooting

Pythian, may you come bringing prosperity to this city, sending to a people without grief Peace flourishing with Order [Eunomia]'. Here compare Hesiod's description at *Works and Days* 901-2, 'Next Zeus married radiant Themis, who bore the Hours, Order [Eunomia] and Justice [Dike] and blooming Peace [Eirene]'.

Pausanias (1.8.2, 9.16.2) saw a statue of Peace holding the child Wealth in the Athenian agora by the sculptor Cephisodotus, who belongs to the earlier part of the fourth century.[8] The statue may be somewhat later than the establishment of the cult of Peace. A copy of Cephisodotus' fourth-century original has survived in a fine Roman copy, now in the Munich Glyptothek (cover photo). This shows a maternal Peace with the young child Wealth on her arm and neatly combines the associations of Peace with wealth and prosperity and with her epithet, 'nurse of young men'.[9]

But what sort of figure was wheeled out of the central doors and later formally installed to preside over the action? At 615-18, Trygaeus and the chorus play on two meanings of the verb *prosēkein* ('to have a connection with', 'to be related to'):

TRYG: I have never heard that from anyone before, no by Apollo, that
    Pheidias had some connection with Peace.
CHOR: Nor I, not until just now. That's why she's so fair to look at –
    she's his kinswoman. There's a lot we don't know.

Pheidias was famous for the beauty of his sculptures on the buildings on the Acropolis. This suggests that the statue of Peace that is dragged into place before the spectators was attractive to look at. But Slater (2002: 123) has suggested that all that was needed would be a pole draped with a woman's robe and an attractive female mask at the top.[10] This would account for what Trygaeus says about her beauty (617-18). If this primitive rendering of Peace evoked laughter, rather than awe, this might explain why Eupolis and Platon could have fun of Aristophanes for his *kolossikon* in *Peace*. It was Aristophanes' purpose not to make Peace a figure of fun and exploitation like the female personifications elsewhere in his comedies, but a solemn and august character. A silent actor playing the role 'would render Peace ... a figure of fun rather than an object of desire. Only as an object ... can Peace have the dignity that the plot requires.'

By the late first century BCE, Rome had made Pax, the Latin equivalent to Eirene (Peace), into a goddess with a cult, places of worship, and a visual iconography on coins and statues. But whereas the Greek *eirēnē* has the overtones of tranquillity and ease, for the Romans *pax* is related to words meaning 'fix by agreement' and is something concrete, achieved through force of arms and a negotiated contract of *fides* ('faith', 'trust'). The early years of the reign of Augustus (27 BCE– 14 CE) celebrated the establishment of peace after a century of civil strife. But this was a 'political' peace, one intimately bound up with the imperial propaganda for Augustus' new regime. Ovid in the first of his *Fasti*, poems celebrating red-letter days in the Roman calendar, addresses Peace, 'Our song has brought us to the altar of Peace ... be present here, Peace, your hair neatly arranged with the laurels of Actium, and remain as a gentle presence to all the world' (1.709–12). The 'laurels of Actium' refer to Augustus' decisive victory over Antony and Cleopatra at Actium in 31 BCE. A Roman peace is thus achieved through military might.

Augustus himself in his *Res Gestae* ('Exploits' – ch. 12) describes how a grateful Senate on his return to Rome in 13 BCE commissioned the consecration of an altar to 'Augustus' Peace' (*pax augusta*). Now known as the Ara Pacis ('Altar of Peace'), it has largely survived, and one panel shows a seated female figure, holding two boys, one very much in the manner of Cephisodotus' Peace. Plants and animals appear around her as symbols of fertility and prosperity. Some have seen her as Tellus ('Earth'), but the prevailing identification is for Pax (Peace). Surrounding panels show that this altar is very much concerned with Rome's history and her present status in the world.[11] Two passages from contemporary poems will suffice to reinforce this political view of Roman peace: 'Let a soldier carry arms only against who threaten with arms, and let the trumpet play only in procession. May the world near and far tremble at the descendants of Aeneas' (Ovid *Fasti* 1.713–15), and Aeneas' vision in the underworld of Rome's future mission in the world, 'Romans, these will be your arts. Remember to rule the peoples of the world by your authority, to impose the custom of peace, to spare the vanquished and to wear down the proud' (Vergil *Aeneid* 6.851–3). Later the first of the Flavian emperors, Vespasian, who came to the throne in 69 CE after an intense year of internal conflict, constructed his own splendid 'temple of Peace' in the centre of Rome to celebrate both the return of peace and his ascension to power.[12] While in Aristophanes' comedy peace is achieved by the ordinary folk and in spite of the political leaders, the Romans owed their experience of Pax to the exploits of their military leaders and eventual rulers.

Recurring images in *Peace*

In Aristophanes metaphors take on flesh and become more than verbal creations. In *Acharnians* the word *spondai* means both 'liquid libation' and 'truce', and so the treaties brought back from Sparta are expressed as vintages of wine (186–200) and the theme of wine and drinking will dominate the rest of the play. War is presented as an unwelcome and ill-behaved guest at a drinking party (977–85) and at the end of the comedy the priest of Dionysus invites Dicaeopolis to dinner from which he returns inebriated and clutching a wine-skin. At *Knights* 1015–27, Paphlagon (Cleon) identifies himself as 'the dog' in an oracle of doubtful authenticity, quite likely a description he adopted in real-life. Accordingly, in *Wasps*, Cleon appears in the trial scene as 'the dog [*kyōn*] from Cydathenaeon'. In *Lysistrata*, the women's tactic to achieve an end to the War is to withhold sex from their husbands; the recurring image in the play is the erect male phallus. Such dominant images are a significant part of Aristophanes' dramatic art.

Perhaps the most striking image in *Peace* is that of smells and odours. At first there is the stench of the excrement being fed to the beetle and the slaves' desire for noses without nostrils, then the foul smell from the creature itself, the references to privies and back alleys, to breaking wind and bowel movements. The jokes about foul smells run their course by the end of the prologue, but Tordoff (2011) shows that they do not vanish altogether, but are applied to unpleasant or hostile characters in the second half of the play, such Cleon's 'stench of a seal ... and camel's arsehole' (758), or Carcinus' family being 'dung pellets' (790), Melanthius and his brother whose 'armpits smell like goats' (812), the cowardly taxiarch who soils himself at the first sign of battle (1175–6), and the new use of a war-helmet as a chamber-pot (1226–8). When Peace emerges along with her attendants, it is their fragrance that immediately attracts Trygaeus (525–38):

> TRYG: What a fragrance you breathe! Sweet, straight to my heart. Ravishing, like perfume and war's end.
> HERMES: So that's not the smell from a soldier's kit-bag?
> TRYG: 'I abhor that hateful gear of that hateful man'. He reeks of onions and indigestion. But she smells of the harvest, of hospitality, the feasts of Dionysus, pipes, performers in tragedy, the lyrics of Sophocles, thrushes, little verses from Euripides ... ivy, wine-strainers, bleating sheep, the bosoms of women rushing back to the country, an empty wine-jar, and many other good things.

War and life in the city are seen in terms of dirt and bad smells, while Peace restores a clean and fragrant way of life in the country. Tordoff (2011: 190) sums up the antithesis that the play establishes:

> The scatological material and the offensive odors that accompany it have been pushed to the margins of society along with the practitioners and supporters of warfare; peace has returned, banishing chaos and bringing with it fragrant scents, nourishment, and an ordered community.

Another prominent theme is food. A recurring theme in Old Comedy was an imaginative fantasy about full plates of fine foods. One of the benefits of Dicaeopolis' personal peace with Sparta in *Acharnians* is that goods from hostile countries are now available in his market-place, especially the mouth-watering eels from Lake Copais. A repeated theme of comedies about a utopia back then or out there is that food appears automatically for humans, with no need to work. But in *Peace* the ideal life involves the honest work of tilling the earth and gathering its fruits. This is especially shown in the chorus' prayer at 556–9, 'how gladly do I welcome this day long desired by just men and by farmers. For such a long time now have I wished to greet my vines again and the figs I planted when I was a younger man.' The second *parabasis* is likewise a hymn to the farmer's life in the country, where bounties of the earth are freely available and to be shared with others. Several of Aristophanes' comedies end with a feast, in the case of *Peace* a wedding banquet at Trygaeus' house.

Peace begins with the disgusting feeding of dung-cakes (*mazai*) to the dung-beetle and ends with Trygaeus' invitation to the spectators to join him, for 'you'll be eating cakes'. Whereas *mazai* were barley-cakes of an inferior quality, the cakes for the wedding (*plakountes*) are of a superior sort (869). Through the course of the comedy we encounter the savoury-mash that War is preparing, the offering of meat with which Trygaeus bribes Hermes (192, 378–9), the imagined dinner and drinking-party which a victorious Aristophanes will be invited to join (769–74), the 'agora filled with good things' (999–1015), Hierocles' attempt to filch some meat from the sacrifice, the idyllic description of summer and winter in the countryside (1127–71), Trygaeus' description of the wedding-feast (1192–6), and Lamachus' son singing lines from Homer about withdrawing from battle and feasting instead (1279–86). Not all the references to food are pleasant: Cleon 'eating shit' in the Underworld, Melanthius and his brother described as 'dainty-eating Gorgons, skate-spotting Harpies ... fish-devourers' (810–15), and Ariphrades volunteering to 'lap up her [Holiday's] broth' (885), a reference to his alleged fondness for oral sex.[13] But for the most part one of the great blessings of Peace will be not having to eat the onion-and-cheese diet of war, but the fresh produce of the earth.

Old Comedy was also exuberant about sexuality and fertility. Later cultures were not always comfortable with this and Aristophanes' *Lysistrata* was virtually ignored until the 1960s. Where both tragedy and satyr-drama employed an elevated style of language, comedy was happy to use the ancient equivalent of four-letter-words. At Euripides'

Ion 338, Creousa says that 'one of friends says that she slept with Zeus', the verb here being *meignunai* ('to mingle'), but at Aristophanes' *Women at the Assembly* 524-5 Blepyrus asks bluntly 'can a woman not get fucked without perfume?' Here the verb is the coarse term *binein*. So, we can expect that comedy will not be delicate but rather straightforward about such matters. At the same time both comic poets and their audiences were ready to detect the slightest hint of a sexual innuendo, even without the 'nudge, nudge, wink, wink' of British comic theatre.[14]

The theme first appears just before the *parabasis* when Hermes tells Trygaeus that he is to 'take Harvest to be his wife, live with her in the country, and raise for yourself ... grapes' (706-8). Trygaeus replies by asking his future wife to give him a kiss and then wonders if 'it would do any harm after such a long time to get deeply into Harvest'. In the scene after the *parabasis*, Trygaeus hands Harvest over to his slave to prepare her for their upcoming wedding. When the slave asks if he should give her anything to eat, Trygaeus replies 'no, she won't want to eat either bread or barley-cake, since she's used to licking ambrosia with the gods above' (852-4). The slave gets the last word, 'well then we'll have to find something for her to lick down here as well'.

But it is Holiday who comes in for an extended scene of sexual innuendo (871-908), dismissed by Platnauer (1964: viii) as 'a – mercifully short – scene of obscenity unrelieved by wit'. Part of comedy's wish-fulfilment had to do with plentiful delicious food and the spectators, especially in the straitened times of war, could vicariously participate in the celebrations of Dicaeopolis or Trygaeus. Similarly, the largely male spectators enjoy vicariously Dicaeopolis' antics with the party-girls (*Ach.* 1198-1221) or Philocleon's insistence at *Wasps* 1367-81 that Dardanis the flute-girl is really a standing-torch and that the black region around her middle is really pitch oozing from the central core – a similar joke is made about Holiday at 891-3. The scene consists of suggestions how she should be sexually treated: groping, cunnilinctus, visual leering, a sequence of imaginative wrestling and equestrian metaphors, and ends with a member of the council eagerly receiving Holiday.[15] When Trygaeus mentions her name at 871, his slave exclaims,

'What? This girl here? What are you saying? Is this the Holiday we used to bang on our way to Brauron when we'd had quite a bit to drink?'

A different sort of sexual allusion occurs in the last scene as Trygaeus and the chorus prepare for the formal marriage procession. From the moment that Peace first appeared at line 520, her return has been linked with a return to the countryside and to the fertility of the earth. Trygaeus prays to the gods 'to give wealth to the Greeks, that all of us may grow many crops of barley and much wine, figs to munch, our wives to bear us children, to gather in as we did before all the good things that we have lost, and that the gleaming iron be gone' (1321–8). He then adds, 'Come here, my wife, to the countryside and, pretty one, lie prettily at my side.' The chorus seem to split in two and sing responsively: 'what shall we do to her/what shall we do to her? We'll reap her harvest/we'll reap her harvest' (1337–40). The verb 'reap' is *trygan*, which relates to harvesting fruit, to *tryx* ('new wine'), and the name Trygaeus. Soon after the chorus address the bride and groom, 'and you will live well, with no problems at all, just gathering figs'. That 'figs' can be comic slang for the male and female genitalia is clear at 1351–2, 'his is large and thick, but her fig is sweet'. The implication is that her favours are to be enjoyed by more than the groom.[16] The wedding of Trygaeus and Harvest is thus a symbol for the larger return of fertility now that Peace has been achieved. We appear to have three different sorts of female personality in this comedy: the sexually promiscuous prostitute (Holiday), the formal wife (Harvest), and the virginal and aloof goddess (Peace).

At one point another image of women appears, when Trygaeus at 974–7 begins to address Peace in elevated language following her installation, 'O most awesome goddess, lady Peace, queen of choruses, queen of marriages, accept our sacrifice'. But the response of the slave, or possibly the chorus, lowers the whole tone of the prayer (978–86):

> yes, by Zeus, accept it and do not behave the way adulterous wives do. For they open the house door a bit and peep outside. And when someone notices them, they go right back in. When the man has gone away, they peep back out again. Don't treat us in that way.

Earlier references in the comedy to Peace presenting herself to the Athenians without success (637–8, 665–7) are here inverted to portray Peace as the potentially unfaithful wife teasing passers-by with only a glimpse. This comic stereotype of the unfaithful wife underlies the central scene of *Women at the Festival*, but Trygaeus is quick to take things in another direction, 'No by Zeus, don't, but show yourself in full in a noble fashion to us who are your admirers, who have worn ourselves out for thirteen years now. Break up our battles and tumults, so that we may call you "Lysimache".' Lysimache can be seen as a 'speaking name', 'she who breaks up battles', but there may be more here. There is good evidence that the priestess of Athena Polias at this time was named Lysimache and it has been suggested that she provides the model for Aristophanes' Lysistrata in 411, 'she who breaks up armies'. This allows us to view Peace as either a priestess, a woman famous in her own right and not for being a man's wife, daughter, mother or sister, or by extension as the virgin patron of Athens herself.

Athens and the other Greeks in *Peace*

Aristophanes' comedies are generally concerned with the city and people of Athens. *Birds* may be set in the sky, but the newly created city of Cloudcuckooland is the creation of a clever Athenian and in its execution seems rather like Athens. *Frogs* is set mostly in the Underworld but the reason for Dionysus' journey is to bring back a poet 'to save the city', that is Athens. But in *Lysistrata* 'the salvation of all of Greece lies in the hands of women' (29–30) and wives from all over Greece gather at Athens to plan the sex-strike. In *Wealth*, the moral problem of why the unjust prosper and the just do not affects all Greece, and not just Athens. In *Peace*, Trygaeus claims to be working for all Greeks or Greece (92, 292–5, 435–6) and uses the word *Panhellenes* at 302. Referring to the Greeks as a whole, the term goes back to Hesiod (*Works and Days* 528) and is found in earlier poetry and drama, often (but not always) in a military context. There are also references to 'the Panhellenic Law', including the right of burial for the dead (see Euripides' *Suppliant Women* 526, 672, a play from the late 420s). Was the term 'Panhellenic' in the air during the months leading up to the Peace?

While both *Peace* and *Lysistrata* nod in the direction of Greek unity, for Aristophanes Athens and Sparta are the main players in achieving peace. In *Acharnians* Dicaeopolis sends Amphitheos to Sparta to arrange his personal peace; nothing is said about the other antagonists in the War. A Megarian and a Theban do appear in two intruder-scenes, but as stereotyped figures of fun to be exploited by the more clever Athenian. Lysistrata welcomes women from Boeotia and the Peloponnese (75), mentioning specifically Lampito from Sparta, a woman from Boeotia, and another from Corinth, but the actual reconciliation is achieved later by a delegation of Spartan men coming to Athens. Both sides recall how Athens and Spartans aided each other in the past (1137–56, 1248–61) and the play ends with each other serenading the reconciliation in song. Like the actual Peace of Nicias, *Lysistrata* ends with an agreement between Athens and Sparta 'to hold us together for a long time' (1265). At one point in his argument with the oracle-monger Hierocles Trygaeus asks, 'should we have kept on fighting ... when it was possible for us to make peace and rule Greece between us?' This differs from the chorus' attitude in *Knights* (1330) when they hail the rejuvenated Demos as 'the monarch of Greece and this city' and a few lines later as 'king of the Greeks' (1330–3). Thucydides (5.29.2–3) makes it clear that the Spartan allies suspected that 'the Spartans in collusion with the Athenians wished to enslave them' by this recently concluded peace. Trygaeus and Lysistrata may begin by stressing the Panhellenic motives behind their actions, but in both cases it is Athens and Sparta who matter.

Cassio (1985: 105–18) observed that in *Peace* there are more than a few references to things and people from Ionia. The Ionians were one of the three major ethnic divisions of the classical Greeks, living principally in Attica, the Aegean islands, and the west coast of Asia Minor. Athens considered herself the Ionian mother-city and their common dialect is called Attic-Ionic. At the end of Euripides' play *Ion*, Athena explains how the race of the Ionians will spring from Ion, son of the Athenian princess Creusa and the god Apollo, and will eventually spread from Athens into the islands, taking their name from Ion. In *Peace*, we meet an imagined Ionian in the theatre speaking in the Ionian dialect (43–8), a light boat from Naxos (143), the city of Chios (164–72), a man named Cillicon who had allegedly betrayed a city in Ionia (363), the recently deceased poet Ion of Chios who is now a star in the sky (831–7), a pointed use of a word in the Ionian dialect (923–34), and a reference to the Ionian city of Cyzicus (1176). It is the first of these that raises a problem of interpretation (words in the Ionic dialect are italicized):

> SLAVE B: I expect that by now some know-it-all youngster among the spectators would be saying, 'What's all this? What's this business about a beetle?'
>
> SLAVE A: And there's an Ionian fellow sitting beside him who says, '*I think* it's *an allusion* to Cleon, that *he's* eating *muck* in Hades.'

Why is the other spectator an Ionian? Foreigners were certainly present at the Dionysia, especially since the tribute from the allies, many of them Ionians, was paraded through the theatre at the festival. Aristophanes' defence of his *Acharnians* at the Lenaea of 425 is that 'Cleon will not be able to accuse me of saying bad things about the city with strangers present. For we are by ourselves and this is the contest at the Lenaea, and strangers are not yet present. The tribute isn't here nor our allies from the cities' (502–6). Since the early natural philosophers such as Thales and Anaximander later became known as the 'Ionian School' of philosophy, one suggestion is that the 'know-it-all' Athenian is being contrasted with the Ionian who does 'know it all'. Two problems here. One is that the 'philosopher' gets the joke wrong since the beetle has nothing to do with Cleon, and no contemporary stereotype presented Ionians as intellectual experts. Rosen (1984) argued that the literary genres of iambus or blame-poetry and fable, as found in Aesop and Archilochus, were associated with Ionia and that an Ionian is thus the proper one first to explain a beetle out of Aesop's riddle and then to respond with an abusive comment on Cleon. While there is evidence

for the iambus as an influence on Old Comedy, there is none for a
specifically Ionian association with the fable. I prefer Olson's explanation
(1998: 76–7) that since in 425 Cleon had been responsible for a
significant increase in the allies' tribute, the Ionians' abusive response
in *Peace* expresses his understandable resentment at him, even in death.

Like other Aristophanic plays, *Peace* does mention and indeed make
fun of the allies, often called 'the cities' or 'the islands', many of whom
would have been Ionian-speaking Greeks. Texts of this time stereotyped
Ionians as rich-living, cowardly in war, and effete, not as expert
philosophers or practitioners of blame-poetry or fable.[17] Hermippus'
Soldiers (or *She-Soldiers* – 429?) appears to have had a chorus of Ionian
soldiers, presented as effeminate and hardly good military material.
Eupolis' *Officers* (F 271) has a character (Dionysus?) express his
fondness for Naxian almonds and wine and at F 272 Dionysus is
described as arriving 'with a brass pot and a bathtub, like an Ionian she-
soldier that's just had a child.' Eupolis' *Cities*, often dated to the Dionysia
of 422, had a chorus of cities from the Athenian empire, including
Amorgos, Tenos, Chios and Cyzicus. Finally, Eupolis' *Spongers*, produced
along with *Peace*, featured the sophist Protagoras of Teos, an Ionian city,
as a character. It may well be the case that at this time Athens was
publicly consolidating her position as the mother-city of the Ionians by
purifying the sacred island of Delos (425) and encouraging the allies to
send first-fruits to Eleusis (*IG* i[3] 78),[18] but that *Peace* was particularly
highlighting the Ionian connection does not seem likely. Both the
details of the negotiations and the terms of the treaty and subsequent
alliance make it clear that this was a treaty between Athens and Sparta
with little attention paid to the wishes and needs of their allies. It is
often assumed that Aristophanes and Eupolis in their comedies were
defending the allied states against predatory politicians and in some
cases against Athenian imperialism itself. But a careful reading shows
that comedy tends to reinforce Athens' attitude of superiority towards
those in the 'empire' – see *Acharnians* 633–42, *Wasps* 698–711 and
Eupolis F 245–7 (from his *Cities*). In these last fragments three allied
cities are described in language that can hardly have been found

flattering. In fact, far from advocating for the allies, as earlier scholars had assumed with confidence, in *Peace* Hermes portrays them as opportunists who chafed at paying their tribute, bribed the Spartan leaders to inflame hostilities with Athens, and bought off the demagogues to end their trumped-up charges (619–22).

Breaking the dramatic illusion in *Peace*

Tragedy and Old Comedy were fundamentally different genres of Greek drama, beyond Aristotle's assertion (*Poetics* 6) that the former was *spoudaios* ('serious') and the latter *geloios* ('ridiculous') and that no tragic poet seems to have written comedy and vice-versa.[19] The *Chorēgos* Vase described in the next chapter illustrates well the difference between the elegant costume of tragedy and the cruder dress of comedy and also in the differing masks worn. The language of tragedy is elevated and serious, that of comedy is colloquial and frequently obscene. The rules of tragic metre are much more restrictive than the free-running verse of comedy – comic parodies of tragedy are often marked by an elevation of both language and metre. For the most part tragedies end in disaster, not always death, while Aristophanes' plays usually conclude with the great idea realized and a celebration of that success. Most tragedies take place in a distant world of the past with characters from heroic myth and legend, while the comedies of Eupolis and Aristophanes are set in contemporary Athens with less than heroic protagonists. An important final distinction is that tragedy maintains the dramatic suspension of disbelief while comedy never creates a consistent illusion and frequently reminds the spectators that they are watching a play.

The spectators can be openly addressed in the prologues (*Kn.* 36, *Wasps* 54, *Birds* 30), have their presence referred to (*Frogs* 1–14, *Birds* 785–800), even insulted during the action (*Cl.* 1096–1104, *Peace* 821–3, *Frogs* 274–6). Often in the *parabases* proper they are addressed as *theatai* ('watchers'), especially so at *Cl.* 518–62, which is a direct lecture to them by the poet in the first person singular. They can be co-opted into the action at *Ach.* 496, when Aristophanes re-writes a line from Euripides' *Telephus* to read 'do not be upset with me, men of the theatre'. At *Frogs* 1109–18, the chorus sing in praise of the spectators who can appreciate the subtleties of a contest between two tragic poets – 'each one owns a book and knows what is clever'. Individual members of the audience can be pointed out – the actual target did not actually have to be in the theatre – as at *Wasps* 72–84, *Peace* 883–5 and *Women at the Assembly* 166–8, while the judges are appealed to directly at *Cl.* 1115–30, *Birds* 1101–17 and *Women at the Assembly* 1154–62.

But *Peace* breaks the dramatic illusion more often than any of the extant comedies. As early as line 9 the slave asks any *andres koprologoi* ('dung-collecting men') present to lend a hand in making dung-cakes and questions the audience more generally at 13–14 and 20–1. The spectators are commonly addressed as *andres* ('men') and the words could mean 'you shit-collecting spectators'.[20] After the imaginary conversation between two spectators about the beetle (43–8), the slave explains the plot to the various types of male spectators, starting with the statement 'my master is crazy, not in the way you lot are, but in a new sort of way' (54–5). The flight of the dung-beetle is interrupted by comments to the audience (149–53, 164–72) and at 173–5 to the crane-operator. So too during the scene with War (244–5, 263–4, 276–9) Trygaeus is giving a running commentary to the spectators. The summons at 296–300 will be answered by the chorus, but the actor very likely directed the appeal into the theatre, since these groups sum up nicely the composition of the audience at the Dionysia. After Peace and her handmaidens emerge from the cave, yet another scene in the theatre is imagined (543–9), this time a confrontation between an angry maker of helmet-crests and the makers of hoes and sickles who are quite content. At 658–9 the spectators are drawn into Hermes' narrative about their rejection of Peace some years before – 'she won't speak to the spectators ... all of you listen why she blames you'. In the *parabasis* proper the chorus become spectators at the performance of comedy, dancing, and tragedy.

The scene with Holiday (868–908) brings the spectators even more firmly into the action, first when Trygaeus asks for someone to take and watch over Holiday and the slave imagines that Ariphrades, a noted sexual deviant, has immediately volunteered. Then in a sexually provocative scene, Trygaeus hands Holiday over to a member of the Council. The presiding counsellors for the month would have been sitting in a reserved area at the front and thus a council-member could be easily located by the actor. Not only is the action being directed into the realm of the audience, they are being given custody of a divine handmaiden, symbolic of the freedom to travel without the dangers of wartime. In *Acharnians*, Dicaeopolis arranges a peace for himself alone, but here a gift of Peace is being awarded to the political authorities of Athens. At the subsequent sacrifice and installation of Peace (923–1022) the spectators become worshippers and at 956–72 are showered with barley-grains and sprinkled with lustral water. At 1115 they are invited to share the sacrificial meats and finally at the end of the comedy not only do they witness the wedding procession of Trygaeus and Harvest, but are invited by Trygaeus to follow along. Thus, in *Peace* the spectators become part of the comic drama to share in the peace that is about to be restored after ten years of war. Cassio (1985: 39) concludes that 'attention seems to be concentrated on a point of contact among actors, chorus, and spectators'.[21]

Peace: Some final thoughts

It is commonly thought that *Peace* is meant to celebrate exuberantly the treaty that was about to be signed by Athens and Sparta. Joy is a repeated theme in the play, from the moment that chorus appear at line 301 when they cannot stop dancing from their delight at the prospect of peace: 'I am happy, I am glad, I fart and laugh out loud that I have escaped the shield, even more than old age' (335–6). This continues through the chorus' welcome of Peace at 582–600, 'welcome, welcome, dearest one, your coming has made us so glad', and is especially prominent in the second *parabasis* which opens 'I rejoice, I do rejoice to be rid of helmet, of cheese and onions.' The last words of the comedy are 'rejoice, people, rejoice, and if you come along with me, and you shall eat cakes'. But with the benefit of hindsight we know that this peace encountered ill-will and mistrust on both sides and lasted only eight years. Thucydides (5.17.2) records how four major allies of Sparta opposed the treaty and the subsequent alliance, that the Spartan commander at Amphipolis refused to hand that city back to the Athenians (5.21.3), that Corinth and other cities were stirring up discontent among Sparta's allies, and finally that Athens began to suspect that Sparta was not living up to the agreement (5.25.2–3). Thucydides in fact calls the peace that followed the treaty of 421 'that suspect armistice' (5.26.3).

Much of Aristophanes' fantasy is a nostalgic look backwards, such as the rejuvenation of Demos in *Knights* to the glory of Marathon (1333–4), the end of *Lysistrata* that recalls Spartan-Athenian détente in the past, or the choice of Aeschylus as the victorious poet in *Frogs*. The word 'utopia' was coined by Thomas More in the sixteenth century from the Greek words '*ou*' ('no') and '*topos*' ('place'). Its basic meaning is thus 'nowhere', although modern usage has created a complementary term 'eutopia', from the Greek word '*eu*' ('good'), that is a place of an ideal existence. The utopian creations in Old Comedy include both senses, a fantastic 'no place' in the past or somewhere out there or in the future, where life was or is or will be ideal. For Trygaeus and the chorus at lines 569–600 peace means a return to a past life in the country:

> TRYG: What I want is to go back to the country myself and after so long to break up the earth with my mattock. Remember, men, the former way we lived which Peace provided for us, those dried fruit cakes, figs and myrtle-berries, sweet new wine, the row of violets beside the well, the olive-trees we long for, and for all these speak to this goddess now in thanks.
>
> CHOR: Hail, dearest one, hail. How welcome is your coming to us. I am seized with yearning for you and so strongly do I want to go back to the country. Object of our desires, you were so good to all of us who laboured at a farmer's life. Before in your day we experienced things that were sweet and free and treasured. To people in the

> country you meant porridge and safety. And so the grape-vines and
> young fig-trees and all the other plants will welcome you with a
> joyful smile.

But the experience of the last century shows that war changes things
and there is no simple going back. After the First World War Richard
King wrote in the *Tatler*, 'the mass of men will gladly sacrifice themselves
for the realisation of a better world, but would never again be willing to
sacrifice themselves merely to preserve the old one'.[22] A character in a
novel set in post-war England in 1951 comments: 'before the war is
never coming back … it has become a land of lost content, a story-
land.'[23] But Aristophanes seems deliberately to imagine such a story-
land and we may ask whether he or his audience really expected this
ideal past to return or whether this is part of a dramatic fantasy. Rupert
Brooke's equally nostalgic poem, 'The Old Vicarage: Grantchester,'
adeptly mixes a poignant paean to English country life, including as in
Peace smells and food ('and is there honey still for tea?') with a tongue-
in-cheek tone and derogatory comments about life in Berlin, where
Brooke wrote the poem in 1912, and the residents of certain towns and
villages in Cambridgeshire. The reader is never certain whether Brooke
is being sentimentally nostalgic or deliberately cruel, and a discerning
spectator or reader may equally well wonder how seriously the pastoral
ideal in *Peace* should be taken. Did Aristophanes or those in the theatre
share this optimistic dream, or were there misgivings? Or did both
playwright and spectators just surrender to the spirit of the moment
and enjoy an indulgent engagement with joy, food, drink and sex?

Peace has her opponents in the comedy, but they are not serious
ones. Some Greeks are working less than enthusiastically for her rescue
and are dismissed. The dawning day of Peace is one 'hateful to Lamachus'
(305), who is also removed from the rescue party (473–4), and his son
appears at the end of the play to sing unwelcome martial verses from
Homer (1270–94). But Aristophanes makes fun of Lamachus principally
for his name and his imposing military dress. He poses no serious threat
in the play. When Hierocles the oracle-monger enters, Trygaeus believes

that 'it's clear he's come to make some objection to the treaties' (1048–9), but it is not peace that he objects to but that he, as a professional seer, has not been consulted or invited to share the sacrificial meats. Again, this is no serious opponent and, like so many intruders in Aristophanes, is driven away with the aid of a strong club. That the arms-merchant complains, 'you have totally ruined me, Trygaeus', does not mean that peace comes at an economic price, but like most intruders in comedy, he thoroughly deserves his fate. The scenes after the *parabasis* do not present obstacles to Peace but are rather the consequences of Peace.

Similarly, the scene with the two boys (1265–1304) is not presenting a serious opposition to Peace, but is incidental humour of the moment, exploiting the poetic motif of 'feasting, not fighting.' Boys sang at feasts and symposia, so who would be the welcome and unwelcome singers and what would they sing at a banquet honouring Peace? Of course, Lamachus' son would sing martial verses from Homer's great war epics, and the son of Cleonymus would sing those infamous elegiacs by Archilochus (F 5), in which the poet anti-heroically boasts of having thrown away his shield. Comedy had a running joke at Cleonymus for some act involving a shield that could be construed as cowardly behaviour.[24] That Cleonymus is 'the most loyal friend [to Peace] by far' (673–8) does not automatically add an ironic tone to the comedy in that it is praising a man whom the state would have regarded as a coward and punished by law for *rhipsaspia* (abandoning one's shield on the battlefield). When Trygaeus dismisses the boy, 'I know very well you'll never forget what you sang about the shield, especially with him as a father' (1302–4), this shows that Cleonymus is still a comic target. Nor does the play advocate the avoidance of military service since at 1179–87 while the chorus may be forced to serve in the army, they still do their duty and go off to war and at 1178 are proud of standing firm.

A lasting peace may have been an impossible dream in the real world at Athens in 421, but a treaty was about to be signed and Aristophanes chose to 'accentuate the positive' by creating both a fairy-tale plot about the rescue of Peace from imprisonment by a monster and a nostalgic rural world for the Athenians now that the war has ended. Aristophanes' comedies tend to provide fantastic and unrealistic solutions to the current problems facing Athens. At line 595, for those who lived in the country Peace meant *sōtēria* ('safety'). Safety or salvation from a crisis seems to be a constant theme in Old Comedy and as far as the poets were concerned, Athens was always in crisis.

Staging *Peace*

For many their first (and perhaps only) experience of Greek drama is reading words on a page and we forget that these words were originally part of a performance before an audience. If we had been there at the City Dionysia of 421, what we took away from that performance of *Peace* would be quite different from reading a modern translation. To watch how Trygaeus flew his dung-beetle or how the chorus dragged the statue out of the cave or how a member of the *boulē* responded to having the stage-naked Holiday dropped in his lap or to hear the delivery of the lines, whether straight or with irony or with sarcasm, could bring us closer to what Aristophanes intended in that first production. This is not to say that subsequent producers are bound to follow the original intentions – the whole point of re-staging classical plays from any age is to find new meanings and connections to a later age and a fresh audience. But while one might not go as far as C.S. Lewis who suggested that 'you must, so far as in you lies, become an Achaean chief while reading Homer, a medieval knight while reading Malory, an eighteenth-century Londoner while reading Johnson', it is still an appealing exercise to try to re-imagine the original production in 421.[1]

For evidence we have the ancient theatrical ruins themselves, scenes of performance painted on vases, statues and statuettes of masked players, as well as the texts themselves and the works of ancient commentators to provide some generally agreed details: an outdoor performance, large audiences, a large open area at the base of a hillside, some sort of building behind the playing-area, two side-entrances, masked performers, a distinctive costume for each of tragedy, satyr-drama, and comedy etc. But there are places where we can only guess. We would like to know, for instance, how many doors were used in the fifth-century theatre, how great a load the *mēchanē* or the *ekkyklēma* could bear, whether there was a raised platform in front of the *skēnē*, what happened in the event of bad weather, what was the relationship between the dancing and the spoken words, whether women could (or better, did) attend the theatre, or what did the spectators take for granted about going to the theatre. The aim of this chapter is to acquaint the reader with the conventions of the Athenian theatre in the late fifth century and to present the current state of scholarship about the production of *Peace* in 421.

Conventions of the Greek theatre

When today's tourist or student visits the Theatre of Dionysus in Athens, the remains that one sees are not those of the classical fifth-century theatre that Aristophanes' performers and audiences would have known. At Athens we now see curved rows of stone seating, distinct rising aisles, elaborate and labelled thrones in the front row, an *orchēstra* with a paved stone floor, and the foundations of a raised structure partway across that *orchēstra*. But a theatre in stone was not constructed until the 330s (by Lycurgus) and that raised structure, the so-called Platform of Phaedrus, belongs to the later Roman period. The Athenian theatre of the late fifth century would have had straight benches (*ikria*) on the hillside, an *orchēstra* of packed earth, and a wooden stage building (*skēnē*) behind the playing area. Traditional estimates of the theatre's capacity ranged from fifteen to seventeen thousand, but recent studies propose a smaller number of seats, from four to ten thousand. It is possible, however, that spectators could sit informally on the hillside above the benches and avoid the formal price of admission, two obols – a basic daily wage in the late fifth century. Aristophanes' plays show also that there were certain reserved areas in the *theatron*. At *Frogs* 296–7, a terrified Dionysus asks his priest to protect him from the monsters in the Underworld, and to this day one elegant throne, now placed in the front row, bears the inscription 'of the priest of Dionysus Eleuthereus [Liberator]'. At *Peace*

868–908, Trygaeus formally hands Holiday over to a member of the Council. The drama works best if members of the Council, or at least the *prytaneis* for that month, sat in a separate section.[2]

This was a theatre very different from that of modern experience. Audiences were not a few dozen or a few hundred people in an enclosed indoor space with curtains, ceiling, backdrop, movable scenery, controlled lighting, and special effects to create a realistic illusion. Rather, thousands sat outside during daylight hours with the Attic hillside in the background. Spectators were conscious of themselves as a group and it has been suggested that highly emotional and dramatic scenes in tragedy could elicit an almost electric response from closely packed members of the audience. A similar effect can be imagined for comedy as infectious laughter spread among the spectators. This was not an aesthetic experience for a few, but a public event in the life of Athens. The dramatic festivals were state-sponsored in that the actors were paid from the public treasury and the presiding archon designated wealthy Athenians to act as *chorēgoi*, who paid for the training and rehearsals of the chorus, supplied costumes and props, and hosted a proper after-party. This service was considered equivalent to outfitting a trireme in a time of war.

The classical theatre at Athens consisted of three areas: the *theatron* (the hillside where the spectators sat), the *orchēstra* or 'dancing-place' at the foot of that hill, and the *skēnē*-building at the back. In the later theatres, such as the splendid fourth-century example at Epidaurus, the *orchēstra* is a perfect circle, but in the late fifth century at Athens the *orchēstra* may have been more of a trapezoidal shape, as we find at the regional deme-theatre at Thorikos, with seats in a straight line and mostly directed forward. It is likely that some of the *ikria* ('benches') could be angled to match the contour of the hill. At Argos, however, the remains of the fifth-century stone theatre reveal row-seating in a straight line. In productions before *c.* 460 the *orchēstra* would supply the playing area for both actors and chorus, with walk-on entries (*eisodoi*) from both sides. For later comedy we are told that these *eisodoi* acquired distinct identities, that to the spectators' right (stage left) leading to the city centre or harbour and the opposite (stage right) to a distant setting. The intruder-scenes at *Ach.* 729–959 work well on this distinction. The Megarian (at 729) and the Theban (at 860) entered through the distant *eisodos*, while the bothersome informers (at 818 and Nicarchus at 910) came in from the local side. At *Peace* 819, Trygaeus returns from Olympus by the distant *eisodos*, Hierocles and the other 'intruders' enter through the local one. A character can enter from an *eisodos* and depart through a door in the *skēnē*-building, as the sickle-maker does at lines 1197–1208.

Aeschylus' early tragedies, produced before 460, show no sign of a *skēnē*-building behind the playing area, but his *Agamemnon* (458) depends on the presence of a building with a central door. Thus, the *skēnē*-building was in place by the early 450s and *Agamemnon* was perhaps the first use of this stage feature. It could represent a house, palace, temple, cave, tent or whatever setting was required, and provided a third and sometimes crucial means of entry to the *orchēstra* through its central doors. Tragedies tended to retain a single dramatic setting – Aeschylus' *Eumenides* is a noteworthy exception, where the *skēnē* represents in turn the temple of Apollo at Delphi, the Acropolis at Athens, and finally the Areopagos. Comedy being more unrestrained can change its setting freely. In the prologue of *Frogs*, Dionysus knocks at the door of Heracles' house (35–7), but later the *skēnē* becomes the house of Plouton in the Underworld. *Peace* opens before the house of Trygaeus in Athens, then moves to the palace of Zeus on Olympus (178–9), returning finally at 819 to the house of Trygaeus.

The central opening was wide, probably with double doors that turned inward, through which a wheeled device called the *ekkyklēma* ('roll out device') could be brought forward to display interior scenes. In *Peace* it was likely used to drag the goddess out from her cave, although it is not clear whether the statue remained on it or was installed somewhere else in the playing area. Both this and the other stage device, the *mēchanē*, will be dealt with below. Characters could appear also on the roof of the *skēnē*-building, called the *theologeion* ('place where gods speak'), although its first documented instance occurs in the opening scene of *Agamemnon* (458), where a watchman stationed upon the roof speaks the prologue. Access to the roof was by a ladder or staircase at the back of the building or perhaps through a ladder and trap-door. At the end of Euripides' *Andromache* (1225–30) the goddess Thetis seems to arrive on the *mēchanē* and then step onto the roof. An extraordinary scene at the end of Euripides' *Orestes* (408) displays the simultaneous use of four performance-spaces. The chorus look on from the *orchēstra*, Menelaos and his servants hammer at the closed doors of the *skēnē*-building, Orestes and two others hold Hermione hostage on the roof, while Apollo with the now-deified Helen addresses all below from the *mēchanē*. There is nothing in extant Old Comedy as bold as the dramatic dénouement of this tragedy.

Taplin (1978) aptly described Greek drama as 'theatre of the mind' since it depends more on the imagination of the spectators than on creating realism through special effects. A play will open with a speaker explaining the background and the setting, as in the opening of Menander's comedy *The Grouch*:

> Now **imagine**, people, that the setting lies in Attica, at Phyle, and that the shrine of the Nymphs that I am coming out of belongs to the people of Phyle and those who farm the rocky ground here – it's a well-known place. In the farm-house on my right lives Cnemon, a real misanthrope ... who never speaks to anyone first, except when he passes my shrine (I'm the god Pan).

Notice the key word 'imagine'. The spectators are asked to do the mental work that transforms the acting space into the distant hillside community of Phyle, the three doors into the residences of Cnemon the 'grouch', his step-son (Gorgias), and the shrine of the Nymphs, and to prepare for the entry of the misanthrope, his daughter and step-son, and later in the prologue the rich young man from the city.

The spectators are often told what they need to know, such as the identity of someone coming into the playing-area, as at *Peace* 1043–50:

> TRYG: There's someone approaching over there, wearing a laurel garland.

SLAVE: Who can that be? He does look pretentious, is he a seer?

TRYG: No, by Zeus, that's got to be Hierocles, the oracle-monger from Oreos.

SLAVE: What's he going to say?

TRYG: Well, it's obvious that he's here to say something against Peace.

SLAVE: No, it's the aroma of sacrifice that's attracted him.

Later, at 1265–7, Trygaeus explains that the two boys are coming out of the house to relieve themselves and to practise their songs. Comic choruses would have been more surprising and unpredictable than in tragedy, and in extant Aristophanes the chorus is almost always identified before they appear: the belligerent old Acharnians at *Ach.* 179–85, the initiates at *Frogs* 154–8, and the summoning of the farmers and others at *Peace* 296–300.

Since the actors wore masks, acting through facial expression was not possible – we are too used to spotlights or the camera close-up – and in a large theatre-space any gestures would have to be grandiose and exaggerated. Again, the spectators are told what they are to imagine. At *Lysist.* 7–8 Calonice exclaims, 'why are you so upset, Lysistrata? Don't scowl so, child. Knitting your eyebrows doesn't suit you.' At 1208–9 as the sickle-maker and the potter exit through the central doors, Trygaeus announces the approach of another 'intruder', 'for here comes an arms-dealer, really upset'. Both his identity and his demeanour are thus communicated to the spectators. On occasion a character will pretend to see someone or something in the *theatron*. For example, at lines 883–5 the slave says that he sees Ariphrades offering to take charge of Holiday. While the actor might have been able to locate Ariphrades among the spectators and thus subject him to public embarrassment, the joke works equally well if the audience just imagines the situation.

Changes of scene are also announced, especially if there is no major break in the play, such as a *parabasis*. At *Knights* 746–55, Paphlagon urges Demos (the People) to hold an assembly, to which the Sausage-Seller agrees, 'but anywhere except the Pnyx' (the usual meeting-place of the assembly, to the west of the Acropolis). After a short choral break at 756–60 we are to imagine that the scene is now the Pnyx. The change in metre from the standard iambics to the more formal anapaestic tetrameters aids in making that transition. As Trygaeus' journey on the dung-beetle is coming to an end, he exclaims (177–8), 'but I think I am near the gods now; in fact, I can see the house of Zeus'. Since Trygaeus is probably returning to the same level from which he began, perhaps even to the same doorway, these words prime the spectators' imagination to accept the new stage reality. In the same way, his words at 819–23 not only insult the audience in good Aristophanic fashion, but also confirm the change of location back to earth. With the re-entry of the slave at 824 the action resumes, now back in front of the house of Trygaeus.

How many levels?

Action in the Athenian theatre could take place in several spaces and on several levels. The closing scene in *Orestes* (see above) has characters speaking in four different areas, ranging from the *mēchanē* to the *orchēstra*. Some have proposed that *Peace* was also played on different levels. On this view, since Trygaeus has flown on the dung-beetle up to Olympus, the scenes between Hermes and Trygaeus (178–728) must be played on the *theologeion*, with a backdrop erected thereon to represent the house of Zeus. This further implies that War along with Riot and the enormous mortar also appeared on the upper level. We do know that characters could appear on the *theologeion*, but was there enough room for a more involved scene and could a backdrop be established there with a working doorway, through which multiple characters would enter and leave? Also, scenes on the roof usually occur at the beginning or the end of a drama and do not last long, certainly not the several hundred lines that make up the first half of *Peace* (178–728). At 361, Trygaeus' remark, 'let's see how we can move these stones away', suggests that he is at the mouth of the cave, not looking down from above, and at 469–71 the chorus-leader asks Trygaeus and Hermes to join in the pulling, to which Trygaeus replies, 'I *am* pulling, gripping the rope; I'm really stuck in and very serious about it.' Unless we imagine the chorus-leader throwing a rope or two up to the top of the *skēnē*-building, Trygaeus and Hermes need to be on the same level as the chorus, that is on the ground.

Those who placed the action before the house of Zeus on the upper level and the cave on the lower level, often interpreted the term *kolossikon* used by the Platonic scholiast to *Apology* 19c to be describing a very large statue and concluded that it was brought out horizontally and when stood upright its head reached the roof of the *skēnē*-building. This allowed Hermes standing above to hear Peace's whispers (657–705). Another suggestion had Trygaeus come down (how?) to help the chorus on the lower level drag out Peace while Hermes remained aloft, again assuming a statue large enough so that Hermes could converse with her. An even more implausible explanation also placed the cave, like Trygaeus' house, below, with that of Zeus above, but then imagined that the stones before the cave were piled as high as the upper level so that Hermes and Trygaeus, standing on that level, could aid in their removal and further that the handmaids of Peace used the ladders mentioned in line 69 first to ascend to Trygaeus and later to come down with him.

The simplest staging assumes that the house of Trygaeus, the cave, and the house of Zeus are all located on the ground level of the *orchēstra*. The *mēchanē* will have raised him into view from behind the *skēnē*-building and landed him on the floor of the *orchēstra*, in front of either the central door or a side door (see below). Trygaeus' words at 177–8 inform the spectators that the playing-area now represents the house of Zeus on Olympus. Most earlier reconstructions of the staging depended on assuming that the words in the text were a literal reflection of what the spectators were actually seeing and that we can use these as a guide-book to the staging. But it is more likely that such comments as 'that one down there' (224), the 'heap of stones' (225), and the dismissal of certain members of the chorus (500–7) were aimed at the spectators' imagination. In any case, there are some matters of staging where we do have to suspend judgement. If the *orchēstra* and *skēnē* have become at

177 the home of the gods on Olympus, then how do the chorus reach that height without a squadron of dung-beetles? The chorus does operate outside the dramatic illusion, since they remain in the *orchēstra* after the return of Trygaeus and the goddesses to earth, and when they finish their *parabasis* at 818, they are now before the house of Trygaeus. At 729–30 they make a point of handing over their 'gear' (*skeuē*) to some stage attendants; this may aid in the transition from Olympus to earth.[3] The statue of Peace also remains in place and similarly shifts from Olympus to Athens. The only use of an elevated level comes at lines 82–177 when Trygaeus on his dung-beetle makes his way through the air and converses with the slave and his daughters below before landing back on the ground before the house of the gods.

How many doors?

As noted above, in the prologue of Menander's comedy *The Grouch* (316) the god Pan identifies three distinct dwellings behind the three doors visible to the spectators: the sanctuary of the Nymphs (centre), the house of Cnemon (the title character), and that of Gorgias. All these entrances are used during the comedy; in fact, the central door is the least used of the three. In the fifth century, however, no extant tragedy requires more than one door, but certain passages in Old Comedy seem to indicate more useable doors on stage. Eupolis F 48 (*Autolycus* – 420) reads 'and the three of them live here, each in their own shack'; this does sound like the speaker in a prologue outlining the physical setting. In the prologue of *Clouds*, Strepsiades and his son are sleeping outside their house, from which a slave brings various items and into which the son departs at line 125. At line 94, Strepsiades points out Socrates' 'think-shop' – 'do you see that little door and small house over there?' The scene can be played with only one door and an audience comfortable with that stage convention, but both here and at *Clouds* 789–803, where Socrates re-enters his 'think-shop' and Strepsiades his own house, things run more smoothly with a second door. At the end of *Clouds*, Strepsiades orders a slave to 'bring out' a ladder and hoe as well as a torch to burn down the 'think-shop', rather awkward if his house and the 'think-shop' are represented by the same door.

Peace also seems to require more than one door.[4] The logical location for the cave of Peace (see below) is behind the central door with the *ekkyklēma* employed to bring her into the playing-area. If there is only the one door, then it has to serve also as the entrance to Trygaeus' house, used by the slaves and children in the prologue and again in the later preparations for the sacrifice and the wedding, and also as the house of Zeus (178–728), through which Hermes, War and Riot enter and leave. This presents some awkward moments. For instance, when Trygaeus and the chorus at 361 are beginning to deal with the stones, Hermes appears suddenly to halt the rescue of Peace. If there is only one door, at this point it represents the cave of Peace and Hermes can hardly enter from the cave they are trying to unblock. Sommerstein (1985: 25) avoids this by having Hermes leave at 232, not into the house of Zeus, but off to one side. The actor can then dodge behind the *skēnē*-front and change for his entry as Riot in the next scene, then re-enter here from the side as Hermes. Notice that Hermes does not say at 232 'I'm going inside', as Pheidippides does at *Cl.* 125 (*eiseimi*) or the slave at *Peace* 149 (*eisiōn*). He merely says 'I'm off' (*eimi*).

Also problematic is the exchange between Hermes and Trygaeus at 221–6, when Trygaeus asks Hermes what has happened to Peace:

> HERM: War has thrown her into a deep cavern.
> TRYG: Cavern? What cavern?
> HERM: This one, down there. And do you see all the stones he has
>   heaped on top – you people will never get her out.

If this scene is played before a single door, then Hermes will be pointing back into the entrance that he has just left and from which War and Riot will enter at 236. Hermes can depart through a side-exit at 233, but War and Riot would certainly come through the door identified ten lines earlier as the cave of Peace 'down there'. The presence of stones could also be physically awkward if they blocked or impeded access through a single door. But there may not be that many stones inside the door, or they may exist only as a painted backdrop or they may be totally imaginary. The overall sense, however, is that the cave that Hermes is pointing out lies somewhere else in the playing area. Olson (1998: xlvii) concludes that 'the palace of Zeus is represented by a secondary door to one side of the central door that represents the cave of Peace'. If we want the house of Trygaeus and that of Zeus to be different entities on stage, then we could imagine a three-door *skēnē* (so Sommerstein 1985: xvii), with the central door representing the cave of Peace and two symmetrically flanking doors for the houses of Trygaeus and Zeus. Trygaeus thus flies on the dung-beetle from his house on one side of the *orchēstra* to that of Zeus on the other. If there are only two doors, we have the comically satisfying situation of Trygaeus flying from and to the same door, now with a different identity.

It all depends on the dramatic conditions and the expectations of the fifth-century audience. If there were only one door, then the play can be made to work, but with some awkward moments to be skirted.[5] But one final point needs to be considered: if the *skēnē*-front in 421 could have two or three distinct doors, why does no extant tragedy seem to take advantage of them? Dover (1966: 7) makes the point, 'when a building is constructed to meet two different purposes, one of which requires only part of what the other requires, it is normal practice and common sense to meet the purpose for which the requirements are more numerous'. Might this have been another difference between the conventions of comedy and tragedy? Though not required anywhere else in extant fifth-century drama, more than one door in the *skēnē* seems to be expected in *Peace*.

The Cave of Peace

The cave in which War has imprisoned Peace very likely lies behind the central door of the *skēnē*-building. This, however, has not been the only suggestion. Olson (1998: xliv–xlvi) has outlined proposed locations for the cave: (a) a covered pit in the floor of the *orchēstra*, (b) a crawl space beneath a raised platform, (c) behind a large pile of rocks on the floor of the *orchēstra*, and (d) behind the central door of the *skēnē*-building. Mastronarde (1990: 285–6) mentions also an earlier reconstruction on which Hermes and Trygaeus are on the roof of the *skēnē*-building and Peace is hauled up through an interior trapdoor. But how could the chorus have assisted in her appearance? For option (a) support has been found in a statement by Pollux (second century CE) that some theatres possessed an underground passage, called 'the Steps of Charon' that provided access to and from the *orchēstra*, but there is no physical evidence for any subterranean level at the theatre in Athens. Even if there were a raised stage (option b), it is unlikely that there was enough space beneath to place and extract the statue and handmaidens from beneath it and an *orchēstra* littered with stones could interfere with the dramatic performance. Option (c) is the easiest to stage, but perhaps too simple in that so much dramatic action in the text concerns the dragging out of Peace, rather than just removing the rocks and uncovering the statue. It is also a long time for the handmaidens to remain immobile and invisible behind a temporary structure in full view of the *theatron*.

On the fourth option, the *ekkyklēma* was used to extract Peace once the stones were removed. The text describes two distinct actions: the removal of the stones (426–30) and then the drawing out of the statue (459–519), a much longer scene. A key word in the first section is *eisiontes* (427 – 'going in'), which shows that some of the chorus went in through the central doors and began to remove the stones. These may be actual stones or a painted backdrop or just to be imagined as inside the doors. The chorus have brought ropes with them (299) and these can be fastened to the *ekkyklēma* on which the statue and the handmaidens rest. Then the actors and the chorus can engage in their dramatic tug-of-war to bring out the statue finally at 519.

In *Peace*, Aristophanes makes comic fun of the two major 'special effects' available in the fifth-century theatre, the *mēchanē* and the *ekkyklēma*, conventions from tragedy which the dramatic illusion of that genre is supposed to maintain. We are told that the function of the *ekkyklēma* was to make indoor scenes visible to the spectators, such as in tragedy at Euripides' *Heracles* 1028–30 (the bodies of Heracles' wife and children) or *Hippolytus* 808–10 (the dead Phaedra with the suicide note fastened to her wrist). In tragedy, the *ekkyklēma* usually displays interior scenes with dead bodies, but twice in comedy Aristophanes wittily uses the *ekkyklēma* to bring a live tragic poet into the playing-area: Euripides at *Ach.* 404–11, with the wry comment that Euripides has so many crippled characters in his plays because he writes with his feet up on a couch, and Agathon also on a couch at *Women at the Festival* 96. We do not know much about the construction of the *ekkyklēma*. The *kykl-* root implies something like a low wheeled wagon,[6] that would fit through the double doors of the *skēnē*, but we do not know how its wheels and axles operated, the maximum load it could bear – in *Heracles* it has to carry three children and their dead mother – how far it could travel into the *orchēstra*, or how it was braked or anchored. The comic text in *Peace* does not mention wheels or rolling, but since the *ekkyklēma* was part of the theatre's equipment, it does seem the easiest way to get the statue into the playing-area and a convenient method for the chorus to haul her out with their ropes.

At lines 720–6, Trygaeus asks how he will be able to get home, since the dung-beetle has disappeared (see below). Hermes tells him that his route home is 'this way, beside the goddess'. Critics offer two explanations here: (i) that Trygaeus and the handmaidens step past the statue and exit through the central door, and (ii) they pass the statue and leave by a side-exit. In either case they will return after the *parabasis* through the distant *eisodos* into the *orchēstra* which now represents the house of Trygaeus at Athens again.

The flight of the dung-beetle

The other major piece of stage equipment is the *mēchanē* or 'machine'. This was used to convey characters through the air to and from the playing-area and either to land them on the *theologeion* or in the *orchēstra* or to have them converse from above with characters below. It is not restricted to divine beings, although these do arrive at the end of a drama to resolve matters and foretell the future. In tragedy the heroes Bellerophon and Perseus travel through the air,[7] and in comedy Socrates, Trygaeus and 'Euripides' (see below). The *mēchanē* is used at least four times in extant comedy: Trygaeus in *Peace*, Socrates at *Clouds* (218), Iris in *Birds* (1196–1261) and the comic 'Euripides' posing as Perseus in *Women at the Festival* (1098–1102). It is an interesting observation that none of Aristophanes' four or five Lenaea-plays employs the *mēchanē* and that *Clouds*, *Peace*, *Birds* and very probably *Women at the Festival* are all Dionysia-plays. Possible explanations are mere coincidence, that the Lenaea-plays were staged in a different theatre, or that the *mēchanē* was not employed at the earlier festival.[8]

Other ancient names for the *mēchanē* are *geranos* ('crane') or *kradē* ('branch'). Pollux (4.128) states that 'what the *mēchanē* is in tragedy they call the *kradē* in comedy'. In *Clouds*, Socrates is 'the man hanging from the perch (*kremathra*)' (218) and looks down on the gods 'from a wicker-frame (*tarros*)' (226). Both Iris in *Birds* and the comic 'Euripides' in *Women at the Festival* are probably strapped directly to the *mēchanē* itself. This would seem how the device was normally used, to bring a single character, a god or a hero, onto the dramatic scene from above. Clearly in Euripides' *Bellerophon*, the *mēchanē* was fitted out as Pegasus, and certain other tragic appearances involve more than just an actor, Athena in a chariot (*Ion*) and Oceanus on a griffin (*Prometheus Bound*). For Trygaeus' flight the *mēchanē* has been dressed up as a dung-beetle large enough to carry the actor, an indication that it could take more than just a single character. In *Peace*, Trygaeus' journey is marked by starts and stops, the former in the more flowing anapaests and the latter in iambics. Thus, a character could speak while moving and also while still. The jerky rise and fall of the dung-beetle, perhaps harmonized with these metres, would have added to the humour of the performance.

Exactly how the *mēchanē* operated is not clear, but the fourth-century comic poet Antiphanes (F 189) tells of tragic poets who 'when they get stuck in their plays and have nothing more to say, they just raise the *mēchanē* like a finger and this satisfies the spectators'. It is clear from *Peace* that the *mēchanē* had a double pivot, up and down and from side to side, perhaps with as much as a 180-degree sweep. Various reconstructions have been proposed and tried out in performance, but all require a system of winch and pulleys, ropes and a beam. Mastronarde (1990: 290–4) presents a plausible reconstruction:

> the most probable form of the fifth-century theater crane is a counterweighted beam, a sort of asymmetrical seesaw that either pivots on its own fulcrum point or moves up and down only within a pivoting upright. Mechanically, this form corresponds to one of the oldest and most widespread lifting devices used in the Mediterranean, the swing beam or *shadouf* used for raising water.

Pollux (4.128) locates the *mēchanē* 'along the left-hand entrance', but not specifying whose left. The machinery will have been located behind the building, either at ground level or on the roof of a low structure. It will have raised Trygaeus into view from behind the *skēnē*-building, swung him over his house, and then landed him on the floor of the *orchēstra*.

Spectators seated higher up on the hillside will have been able to look down over the *skēnē*-building and see the preparation and the operation of this device. The visible cables and creaking machinery have seemed to some hostile to the serious ethos of tragedy, especially with the assumption that it was both slow and clumsy. But the spectators were willing to participate in the suspension of disbelief and those who enjoyed the visual spectacle would eagerly await a dramatic close to the drama. The sounds made by the preparation of the *mēchanē* may be the ancient comic equivalent of the music track in a modern action film which rises to a crescendo just before the critical moment. Something visually dramatic is about to happen.

As mentioned above, comedy makes fun of the devices which tragedy took seriously. Trygaeus' plea to the machine-operator at 173–5 is not the only occasion on which comedy punctures this dramatic illusion. In F 160 (*Gerytades*) we hear 'the machine-operator should have spun the branch [*kradē*] around as quickly as he could' and at F 192 (*Daedalus*), 'machine-operator, when you want your wheel to leave me up above, say "farewell, light of the sun"'. F 4 of Strattis, who shared Aristophanes' fondness for parodying tragedy, reads 'let the machine-operator get me down from the branch [*kradē*] as soon as he can – I'm turning into a fig'. In another fragment (F 46) Strattis begins the opening scene of his *Phoenician Women*, 'I am Dionysus, associated with thyrsuses, *aulos*-players and revelry. Here I am, trapped by the wickedness of others, hanging on the branch [*kradē*] like a fig'. Plato in his *Cratylus* (425d) picks up Antiphanes' comment (F 189) about how the tragic poets resort to the *mēchanē*, 'like tragic poets, who, when they get into difficulty, get out of trouble by raising gods on the *mēchanē*'. Aristotle seems to have this in mind at *Poetics* 1454a37–b8:

> It is clear that the resolution of the plot should come from the story itself and not, as in *Medea*, from the *mēchanē* . . . The *mēchanē* should be used for matters outside the drama, such as events which happened before that a spectator could not see, or which happened afterward. These need to be predicted or narrated.

When was the dung-beetle removed from the playing-area? Trygaeus and his 'steed' land on Olympus at line 178, but he does not notice its absence until lines 720–2:

> TRYG: Home, beetle, let's fly away home.
> HERM: It's not here, mate.
> TRYG: So where's it gone?
> HERM: It's now yoked under the chariot of Zeus and bears his thunderbolt.

A parallel in comedy is the entry of Socrates on his aerial device at *Cl.* 218, from which he dismounts probably at line 238. In both cases there would be no reason to leave the *mēchanē* visible and it is probably removed very promptly. Admittedly, its departure could distract from whatever is happening in the playing-area and some vigorous exchange between the characters might cover its departure, perhaps the summons and entry of the chorus at lines 292–308.

The Installation of Peace: The platform and the altar

While Peace was not a formally worshipped deity at Athens in the late fifth century, passages from earlier poetry and contemporary drama show that by the late 420s she could be seen as a divine entity. The first known cult of Peace with a statue belongs to the middle of the fourth century,[9] but here Aristophanes formally installs the statue freed from the cave, addresses prayers and offers a sacrifice to her. It might seem ironic that Trygaeus has won Hermes over at 403–15 by falsely accusing the Sun and the Moon of trying to overthrow the Olympian gods and here installs Peace officially as a new goddess. The comedy never reveals whether Zeus and the Olympians will return now that peace has been restored to Greece. If the reason for their departure is the unceasing internecine warfare among the Greeks (203–20), presumably then they might, but Hermes is promised a starring role in the new order at 416–25, 'in *your* honour will we celebrate the Panathenaia and the other ceremonies of the gods'.

The three scenes after the *parabasis* feature the three female figures that Trygaeus has brought back from Olympus. Harvest and Holiday have journeyed with him, re-entering through an *eisodos*, the distant one if that distinction existed in the 420s. The statue of Peace as well as the chorus have made a miraculous change of scene back to earth. After some initial by-play with his slave, Trygaeus first hands over Harvest to be prepared for her wedding to Trygaeus (842–70). A longer scene follows, in which Trygaeus presents Holiday to the Council for their sexual pleasure (871–922). Off-colour innuendos and openly sexual crudities run through both scenes. At 923, the slave asks 'so what do we do next?' and is told 'what else but to install her [Peace] with pots?' A dedication ceremony regularly involved the offering of pots filled with boiled vegetables or a gruel – see *Wealth* 1197–8 and F 256 (*Banqueters*)

– as well as an animal sacrifice and the sharing of the sacrificial meat with those present. This is accompanied by a prayer to the new goddess at 974–1016. The actual sacrifice of the sheep is not completed on stage. Since a similarly avoided sacrifice occurs at *Birds* 848–1057, there might be a comic game of seeing how far they can go before abandoning the sacrifice. Another repeated joke is that a sacrifice attracts intruders who come either for the food or as 'experts' to offer their advice. Here the intruder will be the oracle-monger Hierocles (1044–1126), attracted by the aroma of sacrificial meat.

By the end of the first half of the comedy the statue of Peace has been drawn on the *ekkyklēma* through the central doors into the open view of the spectators. What happens in the second half may seem to be more straightforward than the controversies over how many levels and how many doors were employed in the first part, but understanding the action here depends on two hotly debated issues: (a) the presence of a raised platform in front of the *skēnē*-building, and (b) the location of the altar that Trygaeus discovers at line 942. The number of doors in the *skēnē*-building might also affect the staging of these scenes, but not significantly so.

At many modern productions at Epidaurus spectators will see a low wooden platform in front of the remains of a stone *skēnē*-building, where a few wide steps allow for easy access between the lower level of the *orchēstra* and this elevated area. Many scholars today have confidently assumed that such a raised platform existed in the fifth-century theatre also. This they claim was the 'actors' space', as opposed to the 'chorus's space' down below in the *orchēstra* and that most dramatic scenes involving the actors would be staged here. Two objections may be raised. First, a raised platform would not be very useful in a theatre where most of the spectators looked down at the action, and second, the dramas of the fifth century do not reveal a noticeable separation of chorus and actors. In fact, the two groups interacted as much as they were apart. In *Agamemnon* the chorus rush to the doors of the *skēnē*-building when they hear the king's death-cries. In several plays they surround a figure taking refuge at the central focus of the *orchēstra* (*Eumenides*, *Suppliant Women*, *Acharnians*). In *Eumenides* and *Trojan Women* the chorus enter unusually through the central door of the *skēnē*. Dionysus in *Frogs* can race across the *orchēstra* to appeal for protection from his priest sitting in the front row.

Many scholars set much of the dramatic action in the second half of *Peace* on this raised stage. Presumably the *orchēstra* is left for the songs and dances of the chorus, but in the prayers to Peace by Trygaeus and the chorus (974–1016) it makes more dramatic sense to have the chorus close by the statue that they are addressing and not separated with them in the *orchēstra* and the statue and Trygaeus tucked away at the back by the *skēnē*-building. Rehm has argued persuasively that there is no evidence for a raised platform at this early date and that the most effective place for a critical dramatic scene is at or near the centre of the *orchēstra*.[10] At 961–7, the slave is tossing barley-grains (*krithai*) out over the spectators; this would be very difficult to do from a raised platform close to the building. Surely the slave advances to the front of the *orchēstra* to toss out the *krithai*.

The other issue is whether the fifth-century theatre contained a permanent altar which was part of the formal worship of Dionysus, and if so, where was it placed? Sources from later antiquity use the term *thymelē* ('sacrificial hearth') as synonymous with the theatre and refer to the theatrical competitions as the *thymelikoi agōnes*.[11] It would seem that the presence of a prominent altar to Dionysus caused the theatre to be known as the 'sacrificial hearth'. This hearth they located at the central point of the *orchēstra*. Some modern critics have reconstructed this as a formal structure with steps on which an actor or the chorus-leader could stand and address the spectators from this dominant position. Because this was a working cult altar, it would have been unavailable for use as a stage altar. But since over a dozen extant tragedies require an on-stage altar, this must be placed elsewhere, usually on the alleged raised platform and close to the front of the *skēnē*-building. Rehm (1988: 266–7), however, argued that the proper place for any working altar to Dionysus is at his temple below the theatre and that there is no evidence for a permanent cult altar at the centre of the *orchēstra*. Remove this inviolable working altar and the central point becomes free to become an altar, a tomb, or nothing at all. Several suppliant-scenes in tragedy involve groups surrounding another character at the altar or a statue. These are better staged in the centre of the *orchēstra* rather than in the more restricted space at the back near the *skēnē*-building. In the case of Euripides' *Suppliant Women*, Aethra sits at the altar of the Mother and Daughter at Eleusis, surrounded by the chorus (twelve or fifteen) of Argive mothers. Also present are Adrastus and a sub-chorus of boys (at least five), plus possibly some handmaidens. An altar on a raised stage by the *skēnē* would require twenty players or so at the back of the playing-area with the *orchēstra* empty and unused.

I would agree that either 'there did exist a permanent feature at or near the centre-point of the *orchēstra*' or 'a portable piece of stage furniture' could be installed to serve as whatever was needed in that play.[12] In the latter case for *Peace*, such a temporary altar could have been placed there from the start and ignored by players and audience, as is the tomb of Agamemnon in the second-half of Aeschylus' *Libation-Bearers*, or perhaps brought in by stage-hands after the *parabasis* before the return of Trygaeus. If he has been delivering lines 922–38 in the front part of the *orchēstra*, ending with 'while I provide an altar on which we may perform the sacrifice', he will have turned towards his house – more than one door works much better here – stop and exclaim, 'oh look, an altar outside'. Rehm (1988: 307) sums up his discussion of the staging here, 'the comedy of this scene flourishes in the orchestra; if pulled back to a stage altar near the façade, it can barely breathe'.

The preparation scene (922–1044) seems to be a variation on a single theme: run the poor slave into the ground with one task after another. Twice he is sent inside to bring out the sheep and other items needed for the sacrifice (937, 949); later he takes the sheep back inside (1020) and brings out the innards and the paste. In between he has to circle the altar formally with the lustral water (956–7), hand Trygaeus the sacrificial grain (960), wash his hands (961), throw some barley-grains out to the spectators (962), and splash the lustral water over the chorus

(969). If the house door is some distance from the altar, then there is good humour to be had with a running slave who is never allowed to rest. If the slave has to use a door at the side and if the sacrifice is being conducted at some distance in the *orchēstra*, 'the farther he has to run, the better for the comedy.'[13] At times in this scene Trygaeus and the slave are more of a stand-up comedy duo than master and slave, and often it is the slave who gets the punch lines (as at 847–55, 922–36, 956–73). He is a good forerunner of Xanthias in *Frogs* or Carion in *Wealth*.

To sum up the staging of this scene, the chorus have remained in the *orchēstra* while they sang and danced the *parabasis*. The statue of Peace is visible before the central doors, which could invite the spectators to regard them as the doors to a temple for the goddess.[14] If there is more than one door in use, then no entry or exit is made through these central doors in the second half of the play. There are parallels for this in Aeschylus' *Libation-Bearers*, where the door that was so crucial in *Agamemnon* remains unused for the first half of the following play, and in Euripides' *Suppliant Women* where no character uses the central doors, which represent the gates to the sanctuary of the Mother and Daughter at Eleusis. The house of Zeus, if separate from that of Trygaeus, is also not used in the second half of the play. The action is centred solely on the house of Trygaeus and the playing-area in front. The distant *eisodos* is used for the entry of Trygaeus and the goddesses at 819, the local *eisodos* for the entries of Hierocles (1045), the sickle-maker and the potter (1197), and the arms-dealer (1210) and his companions. Since we are told at 1329 that the closing procession is going 'to the country', it is likely that all leave by the distant *eisodos*.

The actors, their characters and costumes

In his summary of the history of tragedy (*Poetics* 1449a14–19), Aristotle records that Aeschylus added a second actor and then Sophocles the third. He does not specifically mention the first actor (*prōtagonistēs*), but ancient tradition assigns that development to Thespis in the sixth century. In the early 440s, a prize began to be awarded to the first actor in tragedy, for comedy at a later date. For almost all the extant fifth-century tragedies the roles can be divided among three actors; the principal exception is Sophocles' late play, *Oedipus at Colonus*, where for a three-actor division to work, the role of Theseus needs to be played by each actor at some point. A three-actor cast works also for most of the extant plays of Aristophanes, apart from scenes in *Lysistrata* and *Frogs*, where a fourth seems to be needed. *Peace* presents little difficulty in assigning speaking roles among three actors:[15]

First actor: TRYGAEUS

Second actor: SECOND SLAVE, HERMES, RIOT, SICKLE-MAKER

Third actor: FIRST SLAVE, WAR, HIEROCLES, ARMS-DEALER

Extras are needed for the daughters (110–50) and also the two boys at the end (1265–1304). There are a number of silent roles in the comedy: Peace's two handmaidens, Harvest and Holiday; the potter who accompanies the sickle-maker; the helmet-maker and spear-merchant who come in with the arms-dealer; and various other slaves and attendants.

Costumes and masks reveal a major difference between ancient comedy and tragedy.[16] Aristotle (*Poetics* 1449a35–6) speaks of the comic mask as 'twisted and ugly, but not painfully so', and Pollux (4.143) refers briefly to the masks of Old Comedy as 'designed to be rather ridiculous', before going on to describe in detail the various masks employed in later New Comedy. Actors in tragedy for the most part wore more elaborate and serious costumes and lifelike masks – comedy makes much of Euripides' supposed penchant for dressing his noble characters in rags.[17] Comic characters wore the ordinary dress of Athenians of the day, but with exaggerated and ridiculous extras such as padding in the shoulders, belly, and buttocks, a grotesque mask, and a dangling phallus.

The best illustration of the difference can be seen on the so-called *Chorēgos*-vase, a bell-*kratēr* from South Italy, *c.* 380 (Figure 5.1).

That this depicts a scene from drama is made clear by the steps leading up to a raised platform and a pair of double-doors in the background. Three comic figures are shown on the right, each with the usual comic padding, phallus, and grotesque mask. One, labelled 'Pyrrhos' (a slave name), is standing on a 'soapbox' gesturing dramatically with his right arm. On either side stand two figures, each labelled '*chorēgos*' (Attic spelling) and dressed similarly. These could be members of the chorus, or the leaders of two half-choruses. On the left immediately in front of the open double-doors stands a figure dressed in the elaborate and elegant tragic costume, holding two spears. He either has no mask or wears a realistic one and is labelled 'Aigisthos'. Clearly this depicts a scene from a comedy about the theatre, specifically about the relationship between tragedy and comedy. The Attic spelling of *chorēgos* steers us in the direction of Old or early Middle Attic comedy; a possible source might be Aristophanes' comedy *Proagon* ('Preview'), produced with *Wasps* at the Lenaea of 422.[18]

Figure 5.1 The *Chorēgos* Vase, Apulian red-figure bell-*kratēr*, *c.* 380.

Masks were employed for a number of reasons. A cast with only three actors meant that an actor would play more than one part and could re-appear, often after a brief interval, with his new role easily appreciated. Masks indicated the difference between males and females, the former usually dark-red in colour and women white, and between young and old, bearded as opposed to clean-shaven, dark hair as against grey or white hair. Allegedly effeminate males or those who, like the students of Socrates, spent most of the time indoors could wear a white or pale mask to distinguish them from 'real men'. *Women at the Assembly* 64 makes this convention clear when one woman explains that she has been sitting out in the sun to make her skin darker like a man. Exaggerated decorated masks and distinctive costumes would assist spectators sitting at a distance to see and identify those coming on-stage, even without the assistance of a verbal cue, such as 'here comes an angry arms-dealer' (1208).

To take the second actor in *Peace*, he appears first as a slave with a dark-coloured (male) mask and the plain dress that suits his status. He explains the dramatic situation to the spectators (50–81), attempts to talk down his master (82–113), and finally goes into the house with Trygaeus' daughters (148). He soon returns as Hermes (180), but wearing a younger mask and a more splendid robe, and perhaps with some of the familiar accoutrements of Hermes. He leaves by a side-exit at 233, then after another quick change (22 lines) re-enters as Riot, with a more terrifying mask and perhaps the same slave's outfit that he wore at the start. War and Riot go back inside at line 288, giving the actor ample time to change for his re-appearance as Hermes at line 361. He remains with Trygaeus and the chorus until the actors depart at line 733. His final appearance comes at 1196 as the sickle-maker, carrying the implements of his trade. As a citizen-male he would be better dressed than in his slave role, perhaps as the metal-smith that he is, but possibly, as Olson (1998: 297) suggests, decked out for the wedding, for which he and the potter have brought contributions (1205–6) and to which they are admitted at 1207–8.

A character's costume could change during the play. In *Birds*, Peisetaerus leaves at 675, clad presumably in the travelling dress of an elderly Athenian male, and returns after the *parabasis* at 801, where the byplay with Euelpides shows that he is now wearing wings over that costume. Later at 1693, he calls for a 'wedding cloak'. In view of the messenger's description at 1708–19, 'here he comes more brilliant than any shining star in its golden course', it is very likely that he is now wearing a brightly coloured robe when he re-enters at 1718. When Demos comes back on stage at *Knights* 1331, the Sausage-Seller describes him as *lampros* ('splendid'), dressed in the old aristocratic fashion of sixty years before. Earlier in the play he would have appeared as a decrepit and ill-dressed old man, but here he has undergone a vast physical change. Line 1321, 'I have boiled him down for you and made *kalos* instead ugly', suggests that Demos has exchanged the bearded old man's mask for the youthful mask of a *kalos*, a word for attractive young male. In both these passages the spectators are prepared for the main character's change of costume by these introductions. So too Trygaeus will appear at 1192 as a splendidly dressed groom preparing for his wedding feast.

Aristophanes' comedy relies on props far more than does tragedy, especially in his earlier dramas. Physical objects are used sparingly in tragedy, but when they do appear, they usually possess a significant dramatic value, such as the purple carpet in *Agamemnon*, the bow of Heracles in *Philoctetes*, or Phaedra's suicide note in *Hippolytus*. To enumerate the more than fifty items referred to or implied by the text of *Peace* would be superfluous, but we can mention the kneading-trough that provides the arresting start to the play; War's giant mixing-bowl and ingredients; the implements that the chorus bring to rescue Peace, which are removed at 729–31; a stage altar and all the preparations for the sacrifice, including a sheep; and the implements of the sickle-maker, potter, arms-dealer etc. There must have been a lot of stage business that the text only hints at and more than a few supernumerary characters bringing items in and out, such as the attendants who remove the chorus's *skeuē* at 729–31 or distribute torches at 1316–17. Plato makes a revealing comment about those who are involved in the pursuit of *mousikē*, 'poets and their assistants, rhapsodes, actors, chorus-members, construction crew, and the makers of all sorts of props [*skeuē*], especially those who deal with women's costume' (*Republic* 373b-c).

In his essay *The Fame of the Athenians* (*Moralia* 348d) Plutarch (late first century CE) compares the exploits of the classical Athenians in culture (*sophia*) and in war (*polemos*), dismissing the achievements, though splendid and entertaining, of the tragic poets as *paidia* ('child's play'). At one point he imagines a parade of tragic poets – he names Euripides, Sophocles, and Aeschylus in particular:

> Do you people want us to bring them [*eisagein*] on carrying the insignia and emblems of their achievements and to grant to each their own entrance [*parodos*]? So then let the poets approach, speaking and singing to the accompaniment of pipes and lyres:
>
> > 'Anyone must keep silence and stand aside for our chorus, whoever does not understand words like these or does not keep a pure heart and mind, who has not sung or danced in the rituals of the august Muses, or who has not been initiated into the Bacchic rites of bull-eating Cratinus.'
>
> Let them carry also their gear [*skeuai*] and their masks and altars, their stage machines [*mēchanas apo skēnēs*] and revolving sets, and their tripods of victory.

Plutarch is using the vocabulary of the theatre: *eisagein* ('to bring characters on stage'), *parodos* (a synonym for *eisodos*, 'theatrical entrance'), *skeuai* ('gear' or 'props' – used half a dozen times in *Peace*), *prosopeion* ('mask'), *mēchanas apo skēnēs* ('stage machinery'). Although the provision of props and effects would more properly be the responsibility of the *chorēgos*, who is mentioned later for the prestige of his victories, Plutarch assigns the physical props and effects to the poets themselves. The imagined entry song, 'anyone must keep silence ...', comes from the *parodos* of *Frogs* (353–6) and, given his dismissal of tragedy as 'child's play', is more than a little ironic since in *Frogs* a celebrated tragic poet is taken back to Athens 'to save the city.' One hopes that Plutarch was conscious of the irony.

Peace: Poets, Plays and Posterity

Homer and other poets

Intertextuality or 'text talking to text' has become a popular and profitable approach to ancient art and literature. This can be a simple allusion to or a brief quotation from an earlier work; or a more extensive use of a character or a scene, such as the recognition scene in Euripides' *Electra* (215–584) which calls the similar scene in Aeschylus' *Libation-Bearers* into question (164–234); or a very substantial relationship, such as Vergil's profound and pervasive use of Homer in his *Aeneid*. Homer was the foundation of classical Greek culture. His poems were frequently recited, and the performer (rhapsode) was a well-known figure in society, often deferred to as an expert authority, not just on poetry, but on other matters as well. At *Frogs* 1030–6, the comic 'Aeschylus' claims that the great poets are those that benefit society: Orpheus for the Mysteries and forbidding murder, Musaeus for the cure of diseases, Hesiod for the rules of farming, and 'the divine Homer ... because he taught useful things, battle order, courage, soldiers' arms.' This may not be accurate, but it does demonstrate Homer's primary role in Greek culture. In Plato's early dialogue *Ion*, Socrates challenges the assumption that because Homer sings about chariot-driving or medicine, Homer or his performer is therefore an expert about these matters.

After dismissing the arms-dealer at 1264, Trygaeus sees two boys coming out to relieve themselves and to practise their songs for the party. Singing was a common entertainment at drinking-parties, either by the guests themselves, as at *Wasps* 1219–64, or by boys – see *Cl.* 1351–77, *Women at the Assembly* 678–80, and Xenophon *Symp.* 3.1. The first boy, to Trygaeus' disgust, sings verses from Homer about battles and fighting and then identifies himself as the son of Lamachus, and who else but Lamachus' son would sing about war? But Aristophanes uses the reverse technique with the second boy. He is named immediately as the son of Cleonymus, who allegedly behaved badly while on military service. What song will *he* sing? The answer is those (in)famous elegiacs by the early seventh-century poet Archilochus (F 5): 'Some Thracian barbarian now proudly holds my shield, quite a good one, which I abandoned beside a bush, I didn't want to but I saved my life.' The first boy's lines are not actual citations from Homer, but a mixture of lines from heroic epic and a comic pastiche about battles and combat, and even when he switches to a feast scene at 1282–3, it is quickly followed by a return to the battlefield (1287).

More may be going on here than allusions to Homer and Archilochus. Scholars have called attention to an ancient work called the *Certamen* ('contest'), supposedly the record of a legendary contest between the two early epic poets, Homer and Hesiod. The account we possess dates from the second century CE, but is based on an earlier version attributed to Alcidamas in the fourth century BCE.[1] *Peace* is thus earlier than Alcidamas' work, but the tradition of this poetic contest is probably an older one. Three of the epic verses sung by the first boy are found in the *Certamen* as we have it, 1270 ~ chapter 15, 1282–3 ~ chapter 9, and the reason given for Hesiod's eventual victory over Homer is that 'it was right for the poet who encouraged farming and peace to win, not the one whose subject was slaughter and war' (chapter 13). This underscores nicely the theme of *Peace*, and Hesiod's *Works and Days* is a call to life in the countryside like that in the second *parabasis* of *Peace*. Lines 225–37 are especially relevant:

> but for those who give fair judgements to citizens and strangers and do not turn away from what is right, their city blossoms and the people therein bloom. Peace the nurse of young men, is in their land and Zeus the Far-Seer never marks out the pains of war for them ... the earth bears a great livelihood for them ... they enjoy good things all the time. They never need to go on board ships since the grain-giving soil provides them with the fruits of the earth.

Homer is cited also in the intruder-scene with Hierocles the oracle-monger (1090–8). Hierocles was a real person (*PAA* 532080), involved in the conduct of sacrifices at Chalcis on Euboea in 446/5 (*IG* i³ 40.64–6). Although he is said to come 'from Oreos,' an Athenian settlement in northern Euboea, in the late 420s he was active in Athens. Line 1084 implies that he had the honour of dining rights at the *prytaneion*, and he is addressed in Eupolis' *Cities* (F 231) as 'Hierocles, greatest lord of oracle-mongers'. When he appears, the slave calls him a *mantis* ('seer'), an official post at Athens, but Trygaeus dismisses him as 'an oracle-monger' (*chrēsmologos*). This was a collector of older oracles, hence his ready citations of Bacis and the Sibyl, and would seem to be something inferior to a *mantis*. As oracles were usually chanted in dactylic hexameters, the metre of epic poetry, Hierocles and Trygaeus exchange mock oracular responses in this metre (1063–87), the former attributing his prophecies to Bacis, a known *chrēsmōidos* ('oracle-singer') of the sixth century. Trygaeus decides to trump Hierocles' Bacis by citing 'a very fine' prophecy from Homer, a mixture of traditional epic phrases and words of his own creation:

> TRYG: And so they pushed away the hateful cloud of war and chose
> Peace, and installed her with a sacrificial offering. But when the
> thighs were burned up and they had eaten the insides, they poured
> a libation from their cups, and I led the way. And no-one handed a
> shining cup to the oracle-monger.
> HIER: That's not anything to do with me, because the Sibyl did not
> utter it.
> TRYG: But the wise Homer said something clever, by Zeus, 'any man
> in love with horrible, internal war has no clan, no rights, no hearth'.[2]
> (1090–8)

In this scene a Homer singing about peace and feasting is to be preferred over a pretentious purveyor of oracles.

In the ode and antode of the *parabasis* (775–818) the scholia (cited as Σ) record that three passages are taken from the elevated choral poems of Stesichorus (*c*. 600). The first instance comes at Σ *Peace* 775:

Muse, push away wars and dance with me your friend, celebrating the
marriages of the gods and the feasts of men and the festivals of the
blessed.

775–9

Muse, push away wars, celebrating with me the marriages of the gods
and the feasts of men and the festivals of the blessed.

Stesichorus F 172 Davies-Finglass

Σ *Peace* 797 names Aristophanes' original here as *Oresteia* of Stesichorus,
a choral poem that influenced Aeschylus' later dramatic treatment of
the vengeance of Orestes in *Libation-Bearers*:

The accomplished poet should sing in public such songs of the long-
tressed Graces, when the songs of spring . . .

796–800

We should sing in public such songs of the long-tressed Graces, gently
finding a Phrygian tune when spring draws near.

Stesichorus F 173

Finally Σ *Peace* 800 cites Stesichorus for the original of *Peace* 800:

When the perching swallow pours forth with his voice the songs of
spring
        When at the time of spring the swallow pours forth.

Stesichorus F 174

The scholiast to the first and third passage observes that these are
'interweavings', a blend of original Stesichorus and Aristophanes' own
words.

Although only F 173 is specifically assigned to Stesichorus' *Oresteia*,
all three passages are routinely assigned in collections to that work.
Platnauer (1964: 135) comments that the lines 'do not seem at all
appropriate to an *Oresteia*', since that story told of Orestes' revenge for
the murder of his father, Agamemnon, by killing his own mother and
her lover. But if they are an invocation at the opening of the poem, they
may have little to do with the coming narrative. Aristophanes would
have chosen them because opening lines were better known to the

spectators, for their sentiment of 'pushing away wars' – 'pushing away the hostile cloud of war' (1090) – and because the dramatic festival and the signing of the treaty came in springtime, more reasons to celebrate the swallow's song. All of these three intertextual references, the songs of the boys, trading oracles with Hierocles, and the citations from Stesichorus are all chosen for their sub-text of 'make peace, not war'.

One final mention of a poet has little to do with peace, but is a topical joke at Ion of Chios, at 831–7, who wrote in many literary genres, both prose and poetry. Several tragedies are assigned to him, and we know that he finished third at the Dionysia of 428. The exchange shows that he had died recently:

SLAVE: It's not true what they say, that when we die, we become stars in the sky?
TRYG: Oh, but it is.
SLAVE: So who's a star there now?
TRYG: Ion of Chios, who once composed 'The Star of Dawn' here on earth. So when he arrived, everyone started calling him 'Dawn Star.'

Peace and the tragic poets

Most of the intertextual allusions in Aristophanes are to contemporary tragedy, and it has often been observed that Aristophanes defines his own comic genre (*trygōidia*) in relation to tragedy (*tragōidia*). At *Birds* 786–9, one advantage of having wings is that 'if any of you spectators had wings and being hungry and bored with the tragic choruses, he could fly off home, have a nice lunch, and fly back here to us on a full stomach'. In *Frogs*, Aristophanes stages a contest between Aeschylus and Euripides for the throne of tragedy, in which Dionysus complains at 1413 that it is hard to make a judgement since 'I consider one a great poet, and I really like the other'. Since antiquity, scholars have debated which poet is 'great' and which 'the other', but Aristophanes establishes an antithesis between artistic brilliance and the poet's duty to his city. I suspect that Aristophanes in *Frogs* is suggesting that if one wants a poet with both genius and civic duty, look no farther than the comedian you are reading (watching).

The most visually impressive scene in *Peace* is the flight of Trygaeus on the dung-beetle, a parody of an equally striking scene in Euripides' lost tragedy, *Bellerophon*. Since Aristophanes mentioned 'the rags of Bellerophon' previously at *Ach.* 426–8 (in 425), *Bellerophon* must have been produced at the latest in 426, at least five years before *Peace*. Ancient sources explained that he wandered about in rags following his catastrophic fall from Pegasus, and some have imagined that this is how Bellerophon appeared at the end of the play. But an opening appearance as a withdrawn man in rags (compare *Philoctetes*) would have been equally dramatic and thus remembered more distinctly. *Bellerophon* must antedate *Acharnians* (425) and since Euripides' *Medea* (431) seems to be the earliest known use of the *mēchanē*, a date in the early 420s seems likely for the tragedy. *Bellerophon* is usually viewed as a 'sequel' to an earlier play *Stheneboia*, based on the story told in *Iliad* 6, but for both plays the fragments themselves are not all that revealing and we depend on other sources to suggest a plot-line.[3] Some time after the events depicted in *Stheneboia*, Bellerophon is in Lycia, and if F 285 comes from the start of the play, he has had some distress in his life. F 286 contains a strong denial of the gods' existence and F 292 qualifies this objection by insisting that the gods exist, but 'if gods do anything shameful, then they are not gods'. Bellerophon is usually viewed as the speaker of F 286, but his mission to seek out the gods suggests that it is not the existence of the gods that he questions, but their justice. Thus F 286 may have been spoken by a character like the Nurse at *Hippolytus* 490–1, who encourages Phaedra to pursue her step-son – 'what matters is not fine sentiments, but the man'. Critics have offered various explanations of Bellerophon's misfortunes: death of his children, conflict with his father-in-law Iobates, revenge sought by a son of Stheneboia, disillusion with his own life, and his misgivings about the gods. But all events lead up to his decision to fly on Pegasus up to Olympus and confront the gods. The beginning of the flight was staged using the *mēchanē* and he would have then vanished behind the *skēnē-*

building, the opposite of Trygaeus' flight. A messenger-speech would have announced his disastrous fall from Pegasus to earth, and like Hippolytus he was carried on stage in extreme distress, perhaps to die (see F 310–11). A god speaks the final scene, announcing that Pegasus will now be serving the chariot of Zeus (F 312).

Aristophanes' sustained parodies of Euripides focus on dramatic scenes. At *Ach.* 325–57 Dicaeopolis re-enacts briefly a memorable scene from *Telephus* (438) where Telephus holds the baby Orestes hostage at knife-point until he is allowed to speak before the Argives. Here the 'baby' is a charcoal-basket, the point being that Acharnae's principal export was charcoal (see also the chorus' self-description at 665–75). In *Women at the Festival* he selects two vivid moments from Euripides' recent *Andromeda*: Andromeda chained by the sea lamenting her fate with only Echo for company (1008–97), and then the winged arrival of Perseus to her rescue (1098–1135). In the same comedy, Euripides' in-law has staged his own version of the hostage-scene from *Telephus* (688–762) and then at 765–84 re-enacts a scene from *Palamedes* (415), where Palamedes' brother inscribed a desperate message to their father on oar-blades and cast them into the sea. What caught Aristophanes' attention in *Bellerophon* was clearly the dramatic flight on Pegasus. In Euripides' play this scene occurred later in the drama, but Aristophanes has moved it to the prologue, thus providing an arresting and memorable start to his comedy. Trygaeus' reason for his journey is attributed by the slave to madness or bile-fever (65–6), but his questions for Zeus are serious ones and would fit neatly with the debate about the gods in *Bellerophon*. More than one critic has seen in Bellerophon's personality traces of depression and melancholy, especially in F 285, and this may come be reflected in Trygaeus' *mania*.[4]

Comic parody incongruously juxtaposes the serious ethos of tragedy with a ridiculous realism of comedy. Thus, the noble Pegasus becomes a giant dung-beetle from Mount Etna, along with an appropriately disgusting diet. The heroic Bellerophon with a royal ancestry has been replaced by a rough wine-grower from the Athenian countryside. The actual journey is described in a mixture of tragic and comic style. When the beetle is actually in flight (e.g., at 82–101), the characters sing in anapaestic dimeter, found also at F 308–9 of *Bellerophon*, but the switch to the iambic trimeter at 102–13 lowers the tone. The vocabulary can plunge from elevated poetry to the colloquial words of comedy, as when the daughter asks Trygaeus (114–18), 'O father, father, has a truthful tale come to our halls, that you have abandoned me and airborne amongst the birds you will go to blazes. Is any of this really true, father, tell me if you love me at all.'[5] The scholiast informs us that these verses are a parody, not from *Bellerophon*, but from Euripides' notorious *Aeolus* (see *Cl.* 1371–2). Harvey (1971) suggests that the opening scene of *Peace* with a pair of speakers, the description of the main character's *mania*, an off-stage ejaculation, and the presence of children is intended to evoke Euripides' *Medea* (431), which featured a striking use of the *mēchanē* at the end of the play.

Aristophanes' comedies present fantastic solutions to current problems, but underneath the fantasy can we see the comic poet setting his genre up against tragedy, the serious and elevated dramatic form? The stories of Bellerophon and Trygaeus present a man concerned about the relationship between gods and mortals, one of tragedy's major themes, but it is the comic hero who reaches Olympus, finds that the gods have abandoned the Greeks, and solves the problem with the help of other mortals and the connivance of Hermes. Tragedy usually ends in failure and disaster. In *Poetics* chapter 13, Aristotle claims that the best sort of tragedy involves a person 'falling into misfortune', and although Euripides does present plays with a 'happy ending' (such as *Iphigeneia among the Taurians*, *Helen*, *Ion*, and the lost *Andromeda*), in these plays too there is still a potential for disaster. A tragedy about Bellerophon is doomed to end badly, while comedy can provide the successful and satisfying ending.

Several critics have suggested that *Peace* owes something to certain lost satyr-dramas. Most commonly cited is Aeschylus' *Net-Haulers*, possibly part of a tetralogy about the hero Perseus. The play dramatized Danae's arrival on the island of Seriphos, washed ashore in a chest with her infant son Perseus. We have about sixty lines on papyrus (*PSI* 1209,

POxy. 2161) from two scenes later in the play.[6] In the first (F 46a–c), a fisherman and another character, probably Dictys, brother to the local king, sight the chest and summon aid to tow it to land, and in the second (F 47a) Silenus, the leader of the satyrs who have brought the chest ashore, confronts Danae and her infant son and imagines that he has now found a ready-made family. Of relevance to *Peace* is the call for help in landing the chest, which sounds much like Trygaeus' summons at 296-9, 'Come here, all farmers and vine-diggers and if there is a shepherd anywhere in the area and ... you race of charcoal-burners' (F 46a.18–20). It is to this summons that the chorus of satyrs will have responded. In F 46c a character (probably Silenus) calls for further assistance, 'You <inhabitants> of this sea-girt land ... and all you country-people ... run to our aid ... and don't let go of the rope.' As in *Peace*, the hauling has not gone smoothly and adjustments have to be made. At the end of the rope is an attractive female figure, in this case Danae, but she is played by a speaking human actor, who begs Dictys not to hand her over to these creatures. There follows some crude by-play where Silenus imagines the baby stroking his 'shining smooth dome, edged in red', which could be either his bald head or the tip of his stage phallus. This is comparable to the sexual exploitation of Holiday and Harvest in Aristophanes' play.

One may reasonably conclude that Aristophanes knew Aeschylus' satyr-drama and that it did influence the hauling-scene in *Peace*. The summons to various groups, including farmers and vine-diggers, and the subsequent call for further aid sounds like a direct allusion. So how would Aristophanes have known a satyr-drama by a playwright who died fifteen years before he was born? We know that books were being sold at this time and copies of Aeschylus' plays were probably available, for how else could the revivals of the later fifth century have been staged? Perhaps a revival of the Perseus-plays and *Net-Haulers* had been presented in the 420s.

As noted in chapter four, a *kratēr* at Ferrara shows an unnamed female figure partly emerged from the earth, surrounded by cavorting satyrs brandishing mallets (*sphyrai*) and an *aulos*-player.[7] The presence of the piper indicates a public performance, and some have seen this vase as illustrating Sophocles' lost satyr-drama *Pandora or Mallet-Beaters* and further concluded that this satyr-drama influenced Aristophanes' comedy, since at *Peace* 566 one of the implements is a *sphyra*. Bur satyrs with mallets are found on other pots and there is good visual evidence for fertility deities, usually female, rising from the ground. The dragging out of Peace probably has more in common with this ritual pattern than with a particular satyr-drama by Sophocles.

Some have seen in Trygaeus a human counterpart to Prometheus, who brought fire for humanity from Olympus to create a stable and civilized way of life on earth. Like Prometheus, Trygaeus is hostile to Zeus and the Olympian gods and stands alone as a benefactor of humanity by bringing a divine gift down to humanity. We do possess an extant tragedy, *Prometheus Bound*, traditionally assigned to Aeschylus, although recent scholarship prefers a date in the 430s and an authorship other than Aeschylus. Hermes does appear in both plays as a lackey to the gods and hostile to humanity and to their champion, but while there may be a few phrases in common between *Prometheus Bound* and *Peace*, there is nothing to suggest any actual influence.[8] If a dramatic version of Prometheus influenced Aristophanes, perhaps it was Aeschylus' satyr-play of 472, *Prometheus Firebringer*, which would have depicted the arrival of Prometheus with his divine gift.

Peace and other dramatic performers

There are few jokes in *Peace* at actual political figures. Five shots at Cleon (47, 270, 313–5, 647–56, 752–9), but he is dead and out of the way, and at 648–50 Trygaeus would like to keep it that way. Lamachus (304, 473–4, 1270–93) is made fun of more for his name and military appearance than for serving as general in that year. Cleonymus (446, 673–8, 1295–1301) may have been an active political figure in the 420s and 410s, responsible for three important decrees involving the allies' tribute in 426/5 (*IG* i³ 61, 68, 69) and especially active during the crises of 415, and although he is paired with Hyperbolus at 670–92, the point is his alleged cowardice in battle, not his politics. The only real political jokes are those at Peisander (395) and Hyperbolus (681–7, 921, 1319).

More poets and playwrights are made fun of in *Peace* than are politicians. At 146–8, Trygaeus' daughter exclaims, 'be careful that you don't slip and plunge down from there, and then being lame you would provide Euripides with a plot-line and become a tragedy'. The sweet smell of Harvest at 530–8 is an interesting blend of country delights and the contemporary festival. These include the Dionysia, pipes, tragic performances, songs of Sophocles and phraselets of Euripides. In the iambic scene that follows Hermes' discourse on the War (657–703) we get a pair of inquiries by Peace about people at Athens over the past decade. In each case two persons are named: first two public figures (Cleonymus and Hyperbolus), and then two well-established dramatists, one tragic (Sophocles) and the other comic (Cratinus).

The reference to Sophocles has puzzled critics since antiquity (695–9):

> HERM: First she asked how Sophocles is doing.
> TRYG: Quite well, but something amazing is happening to him.
> HERM: What?
> TRYG: From Sophocles he's turning into Simonides.
> HERM: Simonides? How so?
> TRYG: Because even though he's old and decrepit, 'for lucre's sake he would set out to sea upon a mat'.

The scholia explain that the poet Simonides was known for writing poems for money and that Sophocles had recently done something that could be so construed. One scholiast suggests that Sophocles had profited financially from his service as a general during the Samian revolt, but Peace is asking about events 'since she left,' i.e. since 431, and the Samian revolt belongs to the early 430s. Sophocles is usually well treated by ancient biographers – see especially the encomium by the comic poet Phrynichus in his *Muses* of 405 (F 32)[9] – and while he did receive a talent for recovering a stolen crown of Athena, he spent it on a shrine of Heracles (*Life of Sophocles* 1.12). Suggestions include a risky business venture, offering inferior dramas to gain a state-sponsored chorus, or a memorable scene from a recent play.

Peace asks also about Cratinus, the grand old man of Attic comedy, who had competed with Aristophanes at the Lenaea of 425 and 424 and at the Dionysia of 423, defeating Aristophanes' *Clouds* on that last occasion with his brilliant comedy *Wine-Flask*. Both poets had been engaged in a running 'feud', the seriousness of which has been debated, but it is most likely that this was all a great game in which poets and spectators each played their parts. At *Kn*. 526–36, Aristophanes praises Cratinus for a brilliant earlier career, but insists that he is now a senile drunkard, well past his prime who should abandon comedy, rest on his laurels, and enjoy free drink in the *prytaneion*. It should be observed that Cratinus is one of Aristophanes' competitors at that festival. Cratinus' alleged fondness for wine was a running stereotype in the comic exchanges and was turned against Aristophanes in *Wine-Flask* when Cratinus, as his own chief character, insisted that drinking wine was essential to creating good comedy.[10] The joke is continued at 700–3:

> HERM: What about the great Cratinus? Is he alive?
> TRYG: He died, when the Spartans invaded.
> HERM: What happened to him?
> TRYG: What happened? He passed away, because he couldn't bear seeing a full jar of wine being smashed.

Since nothing in the remains of Cratinus' plays requires a date after his success with *Wine-Flask* in 423, most assume that Cratinus had died in the previous two years and that Aristophanes is attributing his passing to his alleged fondness for wine. There is a chronological problem with 'when the Spartans invaded', since the Spartans last invaded in 425 and Cratinus was still alive in 423. Aristophanes may just be ignoring chronology to continue the ongoing exchange about Cratinus' drinking habits. Or 'he died' may not be used literally but mean something like our modern use 'I just died', as at *Ach*. 15. More fanciful is the explanation that 'the Spartans' refers to a comedy of that title by Platon, which contained a scene with a broken jar of wine.

In the first five extant comedies, the *parabasis* proper has little to do with the action of the comedy or the identity of the chorus who perform it, and much more with Aristophanes promoting his comic genius and attacking his rivals. At *Ach.* 626–64 he defends his comedy against the attacks of Cleon and shows how his plays benefit the city. At *Kn.* 507–50 he explains why he delayed in producing a comedy under his own name, citing the unfortunate receptions given other comic poets, including Cratinus who competed at the same festival. In *Wasps* (1015–59), after tracing his early career, he demonstrates how he attacks fearsome targets like the Cleon-monster and takes the spectators to task for the failure of *Clouds* the previous year. The text we have of *Clouds* is not that produced at the Dionysia of 423, but an incomplete revision *c.* 419. Part of this revision is a *parabasis* proper (518–62), not in the usual anapaests but in eupolideans, a metre associated with his rival Eupolis who is mentioned at 553–6. Here the poet makes a defence of the comedy that finished third in 423 and of his newer version. In all these passages, Aristophanes adopts the persona of the brilliant but under-appreciated comic poet, who creates original and witty comedy that benefits the city, while his rivals trot out the same unfunny and hackneyed trash.

Peace continues the same line as in *Wasps* the previous year. The chorus begin by stating that the ushers should beat any comic poet who attempts to praise himself in his comedy, *but* if any comic poet deserves to be praised, then he is that comic poet. He has done away with 'such inferior stuff and trash and base buffoonery and created for us [the chorus] a great craft and reared a lofty tower with powerful language and ideas and jokes that are not vulgar' (748–50). Then he again claims the mantle of Heracles and repeats the image of the Cleon-monster from *Wasps* 1029–35. There follows an intriguing passage where he claims that he 'didn't go around the wrestling-grounds trying to pick up boys', a passage which the scholia say is aimed at Eupolis, one of his competing rivals in 421. At 739 he refers to these *antipalous* ('rivals'), which for this festival would have been Eupolis and Leucon, while the *didascalia* reveal Cratinus (425, 424, 423), Ameipsias (423) and Aristomenes (424) as earlier competitors. To these we should add the unknown rivals against whom he was competing with *Banqueters* (427), *Babylonians* (426-D), *Farmers* (424-D?), *Merchant-Ships* (423-L). Possibly Hermippus, Pherecrates, or Platon, all active in the 420s.

The first line of the comedy may refer to another comic rival, when one slave asks the other, 'hand me, hand me quickly a cake for the *kantharos*'. Not until line 7 is the *kantharos* identified as a dung-beetle. Sommerstein (1985: 136) speculated that the spectators might first think *kantharos* to be the comedian Cantharus, victorious at the Dionysia of 422. If the slaves' stage actions give any hint about their disgusting task, then the spectators' first reaction to *kantharos* might be to expect a degrading reference to last year's winner. At 883–5 Trygaeus is preparing to hand Holiday over to a member of the audience. The first to volunteer is identified as Ariphrades, who is known elsewhere (*Kn.* 1280–9, *Wasps* 1275–83) for his fondness for oral sex. That causes Trygaeus to exclaim – 'he'll jump her and lap up her broth'. But Aristotle (*Poetics* 1458b31–59a3) records that there was a comic poet of that name who used to make fun of the language of the tragedians. If this is the case, then Aristophanes' target here is a rival comic poet. Finally, in the opening lines of the *parabasis* proper the chorus warns that 'many thieves lurk around the *skēnē*-buildings and do bad things'. Do these 'thieves' include Aristophanes' rivals who have been allegedly stealing his material?[11]

The ode and antode of the *parabasis* are usually sung in the dramatic personality of the chorus. But at *Peace* 775–818 we get a carefully constructed pair of songs, sung from the viewpoint of dramatic spectators, each beginning and ending with an invocation of the Muse and making fun of two groups of public entertainers. The first to be attacked are Carcinus and his sons (Xenocles, Xenotimus, and a third whose name is variously given). Carcinus himself was a general in the late 430s and also a tragic poet (*TrGF I* 21), whose 'wailing gods' Aristophanes had ridiculed at *Cl.* 1260–1. The efforts of his son

Xenocles, 'the youngest one who writes tragedies' (*Wasps* 1511 – *Tr*GF
I 33), are summarily dismissed at *Women at the Festival* 440–2 and
Frogs 86. Here it is the sons' abilities as dancers that are made fun of, for
at the end of *Wasps* (1498–1537) three dancers respond to Philocleon's
challenge to 'anyone who claims to be a good dancer' to contend with
him in the finale. The slave Xanthias identifies them as the sons of
Carcinus, costumed perhaps as crabs (*karkinos* in Greek means 'crab'),
and at 1519–30 they perform a variety of moves under the direction of
the chorus. At 1531 Carcinus himself ('the lord monarch of the sea')
appears to take pride in his sons' performance. Were these dancers
actually Carcinus and his sons, who were usually described as *tragōidoi*
('performers in tragedy'), or comic dancers pretending to be Carcinus
and his sons?[12] MacDowell (1972: 326–7) proposed that Aristophanes'
dismissal of them at *Peace* 781–95 reflects a poor performance by the
actual sons of Carcinus in the finale of *Wasps*, which in the comedian's
view contributed to that comedy's second-place finish. Certainly, there
is a marked difference between a generally positive attitude toward
the crab-dancers at *Wasps* 1498–1537 and the imaginative insults in
the ode:

> If Carcinus comes along and asks you [Muse] to dance along with his
> sons, do not listen to him or go to assist them. Rather consider them all
> home-grown quails, pygmy-dancers with hedgehog necks, snippets of
> shitballs, gimmick-merchants.

It is certainly in keeping with Aristophanes' superior view of his genre
that one comic actor can take on four tragic performers.

In the antode it is now spring-time (799–800) and the mention of a
chorus (801) shows that the scene is the current Dionysia. The two men
mentioned, Morsimus and Melanthius, are known elsewhere as tragic
poets (*Tr*GF *I* 29, 23), and like Carcinus' dancing sons the Muse is
invited to reject their inferior efforts (809–16):

> when Morsimus and Melanthius do not get choruses, whom [sing.] I
> once heard shrilling out in that piercing voice, when he and his brother
> did get a chorus, that pair of gluttonous Gorgons, skate-spotting

Harpies, wretched scarecrones, with goat-reeking armpits, devourers of all fishes.

The comedians especially make fun of Melanthius' fondness for food. At 1009–15, the chorus imagine him arriving too late to buy any delicacies and singing a lament from his own *Medea.* In Archippus' comedy *Fishes* (*c.* 400) one of the conditions of the treaty between humans and fishes is that Melanthius be handed over to the fishes to be devoured (F 29). It is not certain whether two or three people are attacked here. Morsimus was a member of the family of Aeschylus which produced a number of tragic poets, but there is no evidence that Melanthius also belonged to this family. It is safer to conclude that Melanthius had a brother with whom he produced tragedies. Since Melanthius is made fun of in each of the plays produced at the Dionysia of 421, Eupolis F 178 (*Spongers*) and Leucon F 3 (*Phratry-Members*), he had probably competed at a recent Dionysia or even at the Dionysia of 421. Apart from the reappearance of the Cleon-monster from *Wasps*, these are the most extended passages of personal invective in the play.

Old Comedy in Later Antiquity

Aristophanes' plays were very much tied to a particular city (Athens) at a particular time. Topical humour has a short shelf life; personal jokes and contemporary allusions quickly lose their point and the humour vanishes. Plutarch objects to Old Comedy as entertainment at drinking-parties because each guest would need a learned scholar beside him to explain the jokes (*Moralia* 711f). Thus, any influence a successful comic play might have would be immediate and short-lived. Another factor at work is the change that came over Athenian comedy in the early fourth century. It was not necessarily the advent of a new sort of comedy since some themes and characters which are considered as the hallmarks of Middle Comedy are in fact found in earlier Old Comedy. Rather, it is a change of emphasis owing to a number of factors: the diminishing role of the chorus, the internationalization of comedy, the influence of tragedies of intrigue with a 'happy ending', an altered taste of both audiences and poets, and a different political and social atmosphere following Athens' defeat in the Peloponnesian War. Aristophanes' comedies were not plays for the ages that left an enduring legacy, nor was the fourth century a receptive home for his topical and politically edgy dramas.

A series of fifth- and fourth-century vases, principally from southern Italy, has provided an unusual source of evidence for the immediate afterlife of Old Comedy. Displaying arresting comic scenes with grotesquely costumed performers, these used to be called *phlyax*-vases, named for a crude and vulgar form of performance native to that part of the world. But it has become clear that most of these are illustrating scenes from Athenian Old and Middle Comedy, which contrary to established belief did travel abroad and was performed in the south of Italy. In a few instances we are able to link the vase to a comedy, notably the 'Würzburg Telephus' (*c.* 370) which illustrates a scene from Aristophanes' *Women at the Festival*, a Paestan bell-*kratēr* by Assteas (*c.* 350) showing a scene from Eupolis' *Demes* (417) and an Athenian *oinochoē* (late fifth century) which displays the two principal characters from Eupolis' *Officers*. But for most of these vases we can only guess at what comedy they might be representing and there is no hint of anything that came from *Peace*.[13]

Old Comedy was known and read in the late Roman Republic and into the imperial period, particularly by the Roman satirists (Horace, Persius, Juvenal). Ferriss-Hill (2015) has concluded that Horace and the other satirists had read the poets of Old Comedy, especially the works of the Alexandrian triad, *Eupolis Cratinus Aristophanesque poetae* (*Satires* 1.4.1), and may even have seen plays performed at Rome. Even though Aristophanes was writing comedies for a large audience, principally in the iambic and lyric metres, and Horace is creating satires in the epic hexameter to be read by a more private clientele, Ferriss-Hill (2015) finds a number of points in common between the two genres: a common critical stance, a public defence of their work and a challenge to rivals, personal jokes against real people, the role of the poet as teacher, the persona of the misunderstood poet, striking and inventive language, and a theme of city against country. But Roman satire is not just Old Comedy brought to Rome. Greek comedy did provide ideas, attitudes, language, and characters to Horace and the other Roman satirists, who made a new and distinctly Roman literary genre from that base.

The comic plays were rarely treated as works of literature. Horace (*Art of Poetry* 281–4) admits that Old Comedy was received *non sine multa laude* ('not without much praise'), but immediately points out that its freedom of personal attack had to be curbed by law. Horace (*Satires* 1.4.1–7) and Persius (1.123–5) both praise Old Comedy, but as the ancestor of their own trenchant satires. Perhaps the closest we get to an aesthetic appreciation comes at Quintilian 10.1.65–6 (late first century CE) as part of his 'required reading' for the would-be orator:

> Not only is Old Comedy almost unique for displaying that pure and elegant Attic dialect and also a very fertile freedom of speech. It is especially good at attacking people's faults, but even more it possesses considerable strength in other areas. For it is elevated, elegant, and delightful, and I do not know of any genre . . . closer to oratory or more able to produce orators. There are many writers, but the leading ones are Aristophanes, Eupolis, and Cratinus.

Old Comedy became important in the 'Attic revival' in the second century CE, when it became desirable to write in the purer Attic Greek of the classical age and to seek proper models from that period. In particular the Greek prose writer Lucian (*c.* 120–*c.* 185 CE) possessed an imagination and vocabulary to rival that of Aristophanes, as well as an irreverent sense of humour and a desire to attack rivals and frauds. He admits openly his literary debt to Old Comedy at *Twice-Accused* 33 when a personified Dialogue complains about the way that 'the Syrian [Lucian]' has treated him:

> moreover, he snatched away my respectable tragic mask, and placed another one on me, a comic one, satyr-like, nothing short of ridiculous. Then he went and shut me up with Jest and Iambic and Cynicism and Eupolis and Aristophanes, terribly clever people at cutting up all that is serious and trashing all that is proper.

In *Icaromenippus* Lucian's frequent *alter ego*, the Cynic philosopher Menippus, flies to Olympus to ascertain the exact truth about the gods and their moral relationship with humanity. In chapter 8, Heraclitus is cited for his belief that Polemos (War) is 'father of all things'. Menippus does know (10) Aesop's fable about eagles and beetles being able to reach the gods, but his own solution is to fasten to his body a severed eagle's wing and one from a vulture and to make the ascent himself. On the way there is some by-play involving the Moon and the Sun (20) – cf. *Peace* 406–16 – and finally Menippus encounters Hermes at the door of Heaven (22). But unlike our comedy, Menippus is admitted and has a successful audience with Zeus. There are hints of *Peace* here, but nothing like a concrete allusion.

Other possible references to *Peace* are few and far between in this period. Dion of Prusa (late first century CE) refers to 'the beetles in Attica which have never tasted the best honey in the world, not even if it is poured out before them, but rather the other kind of food' (32.98), but is not sure of the literary source.[14] Letters 7 and 8 of Aelian's *Rustic Letters* (early third century CE) are an exchange of correspondence between a courtesan named Opora ('Harvest') and her lover Dercyllus. A variant on the latter name, Dercylus, is found at *Wasps* 78 and in our comedy Opora is one of the handmaidens of Peace. The writer briefly mentions the division between 'those in the city' and the 'farming folk'[15] and promises to send Opora samples of the country harvest 'figs and bunches of grapes and new-wine (*tryx*) from the vats'. Aelian does quote from Eupolis and Aristophanes in Letter 1, but while themes from *Peace* may underlie Letters 7 and 8, it does not seem to be a direct allusion. If Aelian knew or even read Old Comedy, his was no more than a passing acquaintance.

The modern afterlife of Aristophanes' *Peace*

Old Comedy did not enjoy the same sort of posterity as Greek epic or tragedy. It was the 'New Comedy' of Menander and his contemporaries that would influence later writers of comedy, both ancient and modern.

Aristophanes was known to later ages and had his imitators and devotees, but for the Romans his comic freedom to attack was too dangerous and for Christian-dominated societies his coarse language and openly sexual themes too offensive. Most ancient interest in Aristophanes was scholarly, based (but not exclusively so) at Alexandria, home of the Library and the Mouseion. Aristophanes of Byzantium, a leading scholar of the third century, contributed greatly to establishing the text, identifying problematic passages, and composing the introductory notes which would later become the hypotheses found in the manuscripts of the mediaeval period. Another third-century scholar, Eratosthenes, wrote an influential work in twelve books called *On the Old Comedy*, in which he discussed textual criticism, the authorship of plays, the dates of performances, and the distinctive comic vocabulary. Over the following centuries commentaries to the comedies were written, metrical patterns were identified, and collections of *kōmōidoumenoi* were compiled. In the second and third centuries CE, known for 'the Attic Revival', Old Comedy was held up as an 'approved text' for those who wanted to write in good Attic Greek.

The ancient libraries tried as much as possible to amass a complete collection of the major classical Greek writers. Galen (second century CE) tells two nice stories about how the Library at Alexandria enlarged its collection (*Commentary on Hippocrates'* Epidemics 606–7 Kühn):

> They say that Ptolemy, the king of Egypt, was such a bibliophile that he ordered all the books found on ships arriving at the port to be brought to him. He had copies made on fresh sheets, gave these back to the ship-captains, and the originals which had been brought to him he had deposited in the Library with the inscription 'from the ships.'
>
> His behaviour toward the Athenians is no small indication of how eager he was to collect old books. Giving them a security deposit of fifteen talents, he borrowed the works of Aeschylus, Sophocles, and Euripides on the understanding that he would only copy them and hand back the originals in safe condition. But after having expensive copies made on the finest sheets, he gave these back to Athenians and

kept the books that he had borrowed from them. He urged them to keep the fifteen talents and accept in return the new copies.

Their collection had gaps. Eratosthenes was unsure whether a second version of *Peace* ever existed, confessing himself unable to find a copy in Alexandria, while Crates of Mallus insisted that he had seen a copy. At the Lenaea of 425, Aristophanes' *Acharnians* competed against Cratinus' *Tempest-Tossed* and Eupolis' *New Moons*; the hypothesis records that neither rival comedy had survived. An anonymous writer on comedy (Koster III.18–19) writes of the early comedian Magnes that 'nine plays are attributed to him, but none has survived'.

For each of the dramatists, selections of their plays were made: seven for Aeschylus and Sophocles, and ten for Euripides. But another branch of Euripides' manuscript tradition provides nine further plays from an alphabetical collection, which offers a more representative selection of his works. For Aristophanes the tradition preserved eleven comedies: *Acharnians* (425), *Knights* (424), *Wasps* (422), *Peace* (421), *Clouds*[2] (a partially revised version *c.* 419/8), *Birds* (414), *Lysistrata* (411), *Women at the Festival* (411), *Frogs* (405), *Women at the Assembly* (393–1) and *Wealth* (388). Why were these plays selected? Aristophanes' feud with Cleon would have been well known and could account for the selection of *Acharnians, Knights*, and *Wasps*. *Clouds* featured the revered philosopher Socrates, *Women at the Festival* and *Frogs* had Euripides, well-known figures that would have made these comedies stand out. *Peace* might have been an attractive inclusion for a number of reasons. Cleon is mentioned several times and *Peace* provides the final nail in his coffin. The treaty of 421, highlighted in the fifth book of Thucydides, would also have aroused interest, as would the brilliant parody of Euripides' *Bellerophon*. Among these eleven selected plays were an inner three: *Wealth, Clouds* and *Frogs*, called the 'Byzantine triad', *Clouds* presumably because of Socrates and its philosophic theme, *Frogs* for its debate between the great dramatists, and *Wealth* for offending no-one's delicate sensibilities.

Texts of these eleven plays survived through the tradition of copying and re-copying of manuscripts. In all nearly 200 manuscripts survive containing plays by Aristophanes, most from the later mediaeval period. Our earliest manuscript of Aristophanes is that from Ravenna (R) from the mid-tenth century CE, followed by another good source, the Venetus (V), from the late eleventh century. The manuscript from Ravenna contained seven plays, including *Peace*. *Peace* is found in ten manuscripts, most of which lack lines 948–1011. In 1498, Aldus Manutius published the first printed Greek text of Aristophanes, nine plays including *Peace*, and his edition did include those missing lines. Thereafter, the comedies were frequently re-edited, most attention being paid to recreating the manuscript tradition and to establishing a more accurate text. Nineteenth-century translations were often bowdlerized to lessen indecency and in so doing turned Aristophanes into the ancient equivalent of Gilbert and Sullivan, while in the last century the pendulum swung the other way with colloquial language and risqué themes obscuring the fact this was a formally structured genre composed in verse. For *Peace*, an excellent edition of the scholia (Holwerda 1982), a detailed commentary (Olson 1998), and thoughtful studies embracing literary theory as well as the ancient staging have greatly facilitated the study of this comedy.

Nowhere more than in modern Greece did Aristophanes enjoy a vigorous after-life. As the new Greek state emerged from the war of independence in the 1820s, classical models, especially tragedy, were considered essential to 'the cultural and political advancement of the young state of Hellas' (van Steen 2000: 19). Aristophanes was appreciated as 'most graceful' for his charm and wit and condemned as 'foulmouthed' for his scurrilous language and disregard for moral propriety. Right-wing governments in the last century were especially offended by his political and religious irreverence as well as by his coarse language, but the comic poet remained a favourite of the massed audiences who enthusiastically applauded his plays. This dichotomy was particularly noticeable in the work of the scholar Adamintios Koraes (1748–1833) who laboured greatly to bring Greece into the fold of European culture. He did allow Aristophanes into his canon of recommended ancient texts, but considered only *Wealth* suitable for serious study and maintained that Aristophanes was to be read, not performed. In 1821, he used the rescue of Peace from her cave to illustrate the current plight of Greeks seeking to relight the lamp of classical civilization:

> the lamp that we all wish to relight in Greece, held in darkness, lies deep inside a well. We are but holding the very end of the rope with which we must haul it up. Therefore it is now or never that we must join forces with each other, if we want to prevent the lamp from slipping out of hands.
>
> van Steen 2000: 38

He then cites *Peace* 514–17 where the goddess is first seen emerging from the cave.

Perhaps the most appealing modern Greek adaptation of Aristophanes is Dimitris Potamitis' *The Stories of Grandfather Aristophanes*, first staged in 1979. Described by the author as 'a play for children based on Aristophanes' plays' (Kiritsi 2016: 71), the work consists of five self-contained stories based on *Peace*, *Acharnians*, *Wealth*, *Birds* and *Lysistrata*, accompanied by dancing and music based on Greek folk songs and modern popular tunes. Potamitis' aim in all five episodes is 'the importance of peace and social justice in order for societies to flourish and their citizens to live happily' (Kiritsi 2016: 72).

His opening scene keeps the two slaves preparing disgusting food for the beetle, with the difference that Trygaeus is gorging a tiny beetle to make it grow large enough to carry a rider. A narration by the dramatist himself replaces the exposition of the slave, but the play continues with the exchange between father and daughter, Trygaeus' flight on the beetle, and his encounter with Hermes. War appears to prepare his savoury-mash, with some modern ingredients (and cities) added to the mix. After bribing Hermes with sweets, not meat, and a gold cup, Trygaeus asks the children watching to aid in the rescue of Peace. In an interesting twist Peace refuses to leave her cave, revealing to a child from the audience that she is angry with the Athenians for rejecting her in the past. Like the belief in fairies in *Peter Pan*, Trygaeus' promise that the Athenians will change their ways is put to the children to decide. When they approve, Peace comes out of her prison amid general rejoicing. The only scene from the latter part of Aristophanes' play is the discomfiture of a now bankrupt gun-maker. Above all this is a play aimed at children, with its use of simple music, street slang, and a child's point of view throughout.

Afterlife through productions

Aristophanes' afterlife today lies principally in the frequent restaging of his comedies and his popularity among audiences. *Lysistrata* in particular has enjoyed a great vogue since the 1960s as its twin themes of 'Women in Control' and 'Make Love not War' struck a resonant nerve in modern society.[16] The Archive of Productions of Greek and Roman Drama in Oxford (APGRD) records over 100 productions of *Peace* between 1546 and 2016, in various languages and ranging from amateur productions at schools and universities to fully professional and long-running adaptations.

With a modern production of Aristophanes are we dealing with a 'subsequent staging', a 'translation', a 'version' or an 'adaptation'? The word 'authentic' is often thrown about here, but this supposes that we can at a distance of two and a half millennia make secure assumptions about the ancient conditions of performance and that a modern audience will respond to these. What does a production today need to be 'authentic': outdoor performance, a circular *orchēstra*, masked performers (all male), a large chorus, 'original' props and music, and period costumes? At what point does a modern production cross the line and become a 'version' or an 'adaptation'? When does it cease being Aristophanes' play altogether and become something 'inspired by Aristophanes'?

Nearly a half-century after the publication of the Aldine text in 1498, the first modern production of *Peace* was staged in Greek at Trinity College, Cambridge, in 1546 (APGRD 163). This was directed by the famous scholar-alchemist John Dee whose spectacular machinery for raising Trygaeus on the dung-beetle led people to believe that he had used magic to accomplish this effect (Steggle 2007: 54). Hall (2006: 323) supports the view that this performance may have been the inspiration for a statue of Irene carried in the coronation procession of James I in 1603,[17] accompanied by Quietness (*Hesychia*) and Wealth (*Ploutos*), the latter often associated with Peace in ancient art and literature. Since the Elizabethan and Jacobean ages predominantly associated Aristophanes' comedy with the freedom to attack prominent people of the day, he was grouped with the satirists (Horace, Persius) rather than with the dramatists. Steggle (2007: 61–3) shows how Ben Jonson in his *Poetaster* (1601) goes after two rival poets (Dekker, Marston) in much the same way that Aristophanes attacks his competitors and that his *The Staple of News* contains a trial of a dog like that in *Wasps*. He considers the extended caricature of the contemporary printer Nathaniel Butter 'one of the frankest satirical attacks on a living individual in all extant Renaissance drama'.

The next recorded performances of *Peace* begin in the early twentieth century, but not until the 1960s does the comedy become at all popular – eighteen productions between 1916 and 1959, and then twenty-three in the APGRD data-base for the 1960s. Most modern productions of *Peace* are staged in translation, although some have used the original classical Greek (Cambridge 1546 (APGRD 163), Cambridge Greek Play 1927 (APGRD 841), King's College London Greek Play 1970 (APGRD 1693)). A modern producer or director faces some fundamental problems in putting on a play by Aristophanes. What does one do about the personal jokes and the topical references? A modern reaction is often 'what's the joke' or 'it may have been funny then'. Does one leave them in to preserve the 'authenticity' of the performance or substitute modern equivalents? Michael Ewans's production in Newcastle NSW (2009 (APGRD 14094)), minimalist in terms of staging, retained most of the ancient jokes and depended on timing and excellent comic delivery to deliver the lines, even if the actual point was obscure.[18] Hacks's immensely successful and influential 1962 production in East Germany (APGRD 417) also preserved much of the original action and allusions, while making some structural alterations in the second half. Skilfully steering the line between utopian ideal and the reality of the contemporary regime, the significance of Hacks's production was that 'for the first time the political dimension of Old Comedy was taken seriously on the stage without destroying its comic nature.'[19]

An Israeli production in 1969 (APGRD 7108), however, used Aristophanes' play as a 'kind of libretto, a framework' on which to hang a comedy about Israeli society following the Six-Day War (Yaari 2013: 231). One reviewer described the second part as 'a wonderful current-events satire against chauvinistic fanaticism, fascist demagoguery, and militaristic philosophy'. Claire Kimball produced an extreme adaptation of *Peace* in 2008 (APGRD 14096) in Washington DC, re-staged as *Cows of War* in 2016 (APGRD 14095):

> A Tennessee farmer rides a hot-air balloon to Mount Olympus to persuade the goddess Peace to return to earth. She will, but at a price. Meanwhile, the god War can't understand why he's not more liked, an overjobbed Hermes has to perform five weddings, and a militant vegan veterinary student leads a Chorus of cows into protesting their working conditions on the farm.[20]

The chorus of cows were identically dressed, but each was 'designated by ID numbers that correspond to years of significant wars'.

Handling the chorus and the music is another challenge for the modern producer. In the original there were twenty-four choristers performing along with the actors and their singing and dancing must have been a major part of the ancient performance. Smaller school and university productions may lack both the space for such a large body and sufficient available performers. The Newcastle University production (APGRD 14094) used a small chorus of six, who danced to piped background music or to bongo-drums played by two of the chorus, while the Thiasos production at Austin (APGRD 4394) used eight choristers and off-stage musicians who were sometimes brought into the action.

More professional companies have treated the choral parts of an ancient comedy as something like operetta or Broadway musical, and highlighted the visual and aural effect of these sections. Silk (2007: 293) warns, however, that 'Aristophanic comedy is and remains word-dominant. It is not music-dominant' and one cannot find any exact modern musical equivalent for this aspect of a play by Aristophanes. A *Frogs* produced at Oxford in 1892 (APGRD 572) had music written by Charles Parry, 'which drew on classical and modern Italian opera, Beethoven's symphonies, English airs, popular waltzes and music hall' (Wrigley 2007: 138), while Dennis Arundell's music for the Cambridge Greek Play production of the first part of *Peace* in 1927 (APGRD 841) 'contained some memorable things, such as ... the final chorus'.[21] For a Harvard Student Union production of *Peace* in 1941 (APGRD 7063), a young Leonard Bernstein provided 'a brassy rollicking score' (Massey 2009: 79), which has yet to be published formally. More extreme musical treatments are found in the Judson Poets Theater production by Al Carmines and Lawrence Kornfeld (1969 (APGRD 1747)) with its black-and-white minstrel score, and in a Detroit adaptation in 2002 (APGRD 10014) called 'HeartBEAT,' an 'eclectic blend of pop, R&B, and electrified Beethoven' (Hall 2007: 24).

Peace breaks the dramatic illusion most often in extant Aristophanes, addressing the spectators directly, imagining scenes in the theatre, and bringing the spectators into the action. This element has found its way into some modern productions. Bastin-Hammou (2007: 251) cites Dullin's 1932 *Peace* (APGRD 9694) where the spectators were explicitly invited to assist in dragging out Peace and Vilar's 1961 production (APGRD 416) which blamed the audience as a whole for the loss of Peace. But perhaps the most 'all-inclusive event' among the modern performances of *Peace* is that in 1977 by Karolos Koun [APGRD 1513], who had been staging bold interpretations of Aristophanes since the early 1930s.[22]

For him the experience of the ancient theatre was that of large-scale festive celebrations and he based his productions on 'the assumption that theatre as a festive event could only come into being when both

Figure 6.1 Scene from Karolos Koun's production of *Peace* (Athens 1977), lines 1210–64: Trygaeus and the arms-dealers.

parties, performers and spectators, joined forces' (Varakis 2013: 217). Trygaeus was dressed as a traditional clown with red nose and baggy trousers and the large chorus as rustic peasants. In the 1989 revival (APGRD 1306) a rope being used to drag out Peace was handed to a cabinet minister sitting in the front row, and when Holiday was handed over to the Council, she ended up in that politician's lap. Koun highlighted the sprinkling of barley and water at 956–72 by ensuring that both chorus and spectators were well drenched. After the last line was spoken, there was no defined conclusion, but the communal party continued gradually fading away. His intention was to recreate a popular festival in the countryside, using masks, minor characters with heavy padding and masks, a puppet for Peace, lively folk songs and dances, and above all loud laughter. But more than one reviewer commented that the formal structure of the original was missing and that Aristophanes' text was lost behind the loud and exuberant visual performance. Heydorff's similar production in 1995 (APGRD 9701) was essentially a feast in the countryside, where the spectators were invited to share in the abundant food and drink for all (cf. 1305–31), performances being staged in wine-producing chateaux in the south of France.

Bastin-Hammou (2007: 251) argues that, while the visual aspects of *Peace* provide attractive comic material, most modern productions of the play wish to communicate a serious message on the subject of war and are produced in times of crisis to an audience that needs to hear that message. Michelakis 2002 cites those by Vilar (France – 1961 (APGRD 416), the Algerian crisis), Hacks (East Germany – 1962 (APGRD 417), Cold War), Maréchal (France – 1969 (APGRD 8242)), Vietnam; 1991 (APGRD 8243), Gulf War), Koun (Greece – 1977 (APGRD 1513), fall of the junta), Montes (Colombia – 1995 (APGRD 8244), civil war), and Torrès (France – 1998 (APGRD 9702), 'class strife'). Van Steen (2000: 229) similarly relates the modern Greek productions of 1964 by Katselis (APGRD 420) and Solomos (APGRD 421) to global uncertainty following the assassination of President Kennedy, and those of Bakas (1983 (APGRD 1456)) and Evangelatos (1984–7 (APGRD 1614)) to the renewal of the Cold War in the 1980s. We could add those of Dullin (France – 1932 (APGRD 9694), League of Nations crisis), the Harvard production (1941 (APGRD 7063), possible American entry into the war), Zeks (Israel – 1968 (APGRD 7108), aftermath of the Six-Day War), Carmines (New York – 1969 (APGRD 1747), American race relations), Kleinschmidt (South Africa – 1983 (APGRD 8399)), and Kimball (Washington DC – 2008 (APGRD 14096), 2016 (APGRD 14095), US election years). While Aristophanes' original was produced in a celebratory anticipation of peace, most others are staged in harsher times where peace is a desperately needed solution. Haydn's great Mass in C Major, *Missa in Tempore Belli* ('Mass in Time of War', 1796), is often nicknamed the *Paukenmesse* ('Drum-Roll Mass') from its prominent use of drums in the *Agnus Dei*, implying perhaps that rather than praying 'grant us peace', we should be saying, 'we demand peace'. These modern productions are sending a similar message: war, hatred and divisions now predominate, but a sea-change in attitudes and a genuine desire for something better can lead to a 'peace for our time'.

These last words take us back to the critical negotiations at Munich in September 1938, from which the British Prime Minister, Neville Chamberlain, returned to a hero's welcome first at the airport, then in Downing Street, and later at the Palace. Contemporary reports state that crowds filled the streets in celebration, while customers flocked to shops and department stores, preparing for prosperity and business as usual instead of for war. Theatres and cinemas played to standing-room-only houses and the churches held special services of thanksgiving. Special tributes were paid to Chamberlain and the 'success' of the agreement. Streets were renamed and statues erected in his honour. There were those, however, who were not for rejoicing and one Cabinet minister, Duff Cooper, resigned in protest at what he called 'peace with dishonour'. Can we ask similar questions about the atmosphere at Athens at the time of the Dionysia? Was there still sufficient doubt whether a peace treaty would actually be signed? Does the lack of a dramatic conflict reflect a general assurance among the Athenian populace that peace was just around the corner? Is the play one final plea that the treaty be actually signed? Did Aristophanes, while welcoming the treaty about to be signed, have any doubts about its permanence or is he living happily ever after in an impossible, but dramatically satisfying, dream, set in a nostalgic and idyllic countryside?

Appendix: Was There Another *Peace?*

According to the second hypothesis ancient scholars were uncertain whether there was another play by Aristophanes called 'Peace':

> In the production records Aristophanes is recorded as having similarly produced <another> *Peace*. Eratosthenes [third century] says that it is unclear whether he put on the same play a second time or produced another one which has not been preserved. Crates [third/second century], however, knows of two plays when he writes as follows, 'in *Acharnians* or *Babylonians* or in the other *Peace*'. Also here and there he cites certain verses which are not in the extant version.

Eratosthenes in Alexandria appears to have seen an entry in the production list to 'another *Peace*', but did not have a copy to consult, while Crates at the library in Pergamum claimed to have access to something that he could cite.

Olson (1998: xlix–l) presents five fragments assigned by ancient writers to Aristophanes' *Peace* (F 305–9), but which do not appear in the text that we possess. None is assigned specifically to 'a second' or 'other' *Peace*, such as we have at F 331, 'in the other *Women at the Festival*', at F 335 and 340 ('in the second *Women at the Festival*'), or at F 459 ('in the first *Wealth*'). Three fragments need to be taken seriously (F 305, 306, 308). In the first a speaking character called 'Agriculture' (*Geōrgia*) identifies herself:

> AGRICULTURE: I am the nurse to Peace, dear to all men, her steward, partner, overseer, daughter, sister. I serve her in all these ways.
>
> B: And what is your name?
>
> AGR: My name? Agriculture.

F 306, 'place this shield at once as a covering over the well', also suits a play about Peace – compare *Peace* 1209–64 where Trygaeus finds other uses for the wares of the arms-dealer. The final fragment (F 308) is a single dactylic hexameter, the metre of epic and oracles, 'do not beat the Athenians or else they'll become leather bottles'. This sounds like a mock oracle and the scene with the oracle-monger Hierocles at *Peace* 1043–1126 contains frequent fake oracles in dactylic hexameters.

But do these three fragments ensure the existence of a comedy? I suspect that we have here a case either of misattribution to *Peace* of lines that came from a different comedy or that *Peace* was an alternative title for another comedy by Aristophanes. It need not have been Aristophanes' own title, but the invention of later scholars. The scholia, for example, claim two alternative titles for *Lysistrata*, 'Women at the Adonia' and 'Truces', both derived from references in the play (lines 389, 1114). The most likely candidate is Aristophanes' *Farmers* (*Geōrgoi*), usually dated to the Dionysia of 424, into which a character called 'Agriculture' (*Geōrgia* – F 305) would fit naturally. F 308, the hexameter about the Athenians becoming leather bottles (*molgoi*), seems to be part of a running-joke in comedy. At *Kn.* 963 (424-L) Paphlagon (Cleon disguised) claims that he has an oracle predicting that the People (Demos) must become a *molgos*, a crude word for a wine-skin (*askos*).[1] Aristophanes has substituted here a vulgar word for the wine-skin of the oracle. Finally, the scholiast to *Knights* 963 cites F 103 of *Farmers* for an oracle about the city becoming a *molgos*.

The fragments of *Farmers* suggest that this comedy covered much the same territory as *Peace*. In F 111 the chorus make a wish to Peace very close in spirit to their sentiments in Peace:

> Wealth-deep Peace and little yoke of oxen, how I wish for an end to the war, to dig and dress my vines, after having a bath to draw a draught [*dielkein*] of new wine [*tryx*], to dine on rich bread and cabbage.

The verb *dielkein* usually means 'to drag', but here and *Peace* 1132–3 means 'drain down wine', both passages in a wish by the chorus for the blessings of Peace. The speaker of F 102 is a public official who wants only to return to his farm:

> A: I want to be farming.
> B: So who's stopping you?

A: You people, but suppose I give you a thousand drachmas to let me off my duties.

B: We accept. That's two thousand then with those from Nicias.

The author of the third hypothesis to *Peace* comments that *Peace* 'is not the only play that Aristophanes wrote in support of Peace, but also *Acharnians, Knights,* and *Merchant-Ships*'. Perhaps a scholar's reference to *Farmers* as another 'peace play' was the source of the 'other *Peace*'.

We should note also that the lists of Aristophanes' plays provided by an anonymous writer (Koster XXXa) and by *POxy.* 2659 do designate four comedies as 'second' (*Clouds, Women at the Festival, Aeolosicon, Wealth*), all of which are confirmed from other sources as having had two versions. *Peace* is listed only once. I am thus inclined to think that the 'other *Peace*' did not exist.

Notes

Chapter 1

1　The classical Greeks were divided into three linguistic groups: Dorians, in the west of mainland Greece and also in Sicily and southern Italy; Ionians, of which Athens claimed to be the mother city, in Attica and the central Aegean Sea; and Aeolians, principally in Boeotia and the northeast of the Aegean.

2　The fragments of Epicharmus are collected in *PCG* I, both genuine dramatic remains and a collection of maxims attributed to the comic poet who was regarded as a philosopher of sorts.

3　See Millis and Olson 2012: 156–7.

4　Eupolis' *Demes* probably dates to 417, while the two comedies of Cratinus belong to the 430s.

5　The *parabasis* was a formal feature of Old Comedy, where the chorus addressed spectators often in the plays of the 420s in the voice of the comic poet. See chapter 2.

6　See the appendix for more about *Farmers* and whether it is the 'other *Peace*' mentioned by the second hypothesis to *Peace*.

7　The chorus at *Ach.* 1150–60 complains of the stingy behaviour of a *chorēgos* named Antimachus at the Lenaea of 426. It is not clear whether they are speaking for Aristophanes – in which case we can assign another comedy to an already bursting early career – or for the chorus of some other poet's comedy (more likely).

8　The most recent discussion is that of Biles and Olson 2015: 381–2.

9　Opposing sides of the debate may be found at Luppe 1972 and Storey 2002.

10　Scholia are notes to the texts from the ancient and early mediaeval periods that have been preserved in the manuscript tradition. These also provide useful information in dating both extant and lost comedies.

11　See the thorough discussion by Marshall and van Willigenburg 2004.

12　Athmonon (modern Marousi) was a country deme about eight miles north-east of Athens.

Chapter 2

1 'Catalectic' means that the metrical line lacks its last syllable.
2 Metics (*metoikoi*) were non-Athenians who had permanent residency in Athens. They were not Athenian citizens but did enjoy some rights in law and also many of the responsibilities of citizens. A metic could act as a *chorēgos* at the Lenaea competitions.
3 Revermann (2006: 8–65) in particular challenges this thesis of Taplin.
4 The obvious explanation of the repetition of these lines is that they had been a great hit the previous year, but there are no other confirmed instances of such a practice. It is the last mention of Cleon in *Peace*. See the discussion at Hubbard (1991: 148).
5 The principal manuscripts R and V give lines 978–86 to the slave, but Olson (1998: 256) and Wilson (2007a: 323) assign them to the chorus, partly because a derogative comment about adulterous wives should not be spoken by a slave. But throughout the previous scenes the slave is quick to make off-colour remarks (e.g., 855, 872–80, 891–3) and he and Trygaeus behave less like master and slave and more like a seasoned comedy team.
6 Lamachus was a successful general during the 420s and 410s – Thucydides 6 depicts him as the most capable leader in the expedition to Sicily (415–13) – but he is singled out by the comic poets principally because of his name (La + *machus*), the latter element meaning 'battle'.

Chapter 3

1 While he says that he lived to see the end of the war (404), his formal history breaks off in 411 in the middle of his narrative.
2 Commonly dated to the Dionysia of 422.
3 Olson (1998: 180) offers three explanations of 'smear with garlic', that fighting cocks were fed garlic or rubbed with garlic oil to make them more aggressive, that garlic was a staple of a soldier's diet, or that to 'smear with garlic' is a euphemism for sexual intercourse. In any case Megara was famous for its garlic (246–9).
4 Thucydides mentions only that the Spartans made repeated overtures for peace; it is Aristophanes who provides the number 'three'.

5 This treaty between Athens and Sparta became generally known as the 'Peace of Nicias' (Plut. *Nicias* 9.7); yet Nicias is never mentioned in *Peace*.

6 Used of Cleon at *Peace* 314.

7 Philochorus names the archon for 438/7 as 'Pythodorus' and that for 432/1 as 'Scythodorus' (a name unknown at Athens), but the archons were in fact respectively Theodorus and Pythodorus.

8 Jacoby in *FGrHist* 328 includes the account in Diodorus as F 121 of Ephorus.

9 Nine officials, called 'archons', were appointed annually by lot to run various aspects of the city's administration. The chief archon, the 'eponymous', gave his name to the official year. Thus, *Peace* was produced 'in the archonship of Alcaeus' (422/1, from early July in 422 to late June 421).

10 Thucydides (5.12) dates the battle of Amphipolis 'when the summer was ending'. The scholiast to *Peace* 48 places the battle 'eight months before' the comedy, but that would take us back to August, too early for Thucydides' dating. At 5.20 Thucydides states that his history is operating in terms of 'summers' and 'winters'; thus, mid-October would still be late summer.

11 Might we imagine a sustained parody of the Bellerophon story as told at *Iliad* 6.144–211: the ride of Trygaeus on the dung-beetle to Olympus, followed by a confrontation with Zeus who (either directly or through Hermes) sends him on a mission impossible to rescue Peace from the clutches of War?

12 'Eine *koine eirene* in irgendwelchem Sinne war in den ersten Monaten des Jahres 421 wirklich nicht zu erwartern'.

13 This too might be a reference to the negotiations since Thucydides 5.16.2–3 records that the Spartan king Pleistoanax eagerly supported peace to deflect charges of having taken bribes.

Chapter 4

1 In the 1964 production by the National Theatre of Greece at Epidaurus (APGRD 421), War was costumed as Adolf Hitler, a 'silent anachronism which does not insult nor disrupt the unity of the text' (Diamantopoulos in K. Georgosoupoulos and S. Gogos (2004: 278–9)). Another reviewer (Aim. X) dismissed it as 'a rather cheap laugh'.

2 In Aristophanes' fragments, Dionysus appeared in *Babylonians* (F 75), Agriculture in the 'other *Peace*' (F 305, probably *Farmers*), Calligeneia in the other *Women at the Festival* (F 331) and Poetry in the lost comedy of that name.

3 Illustrations of these vases are found at Bérard (1974), figures 50, 71 and 30 respectively.

4 The name 'Comarchides' means 'leader of the revels' son', an appropriate name for someone planning a party.

5 None of the seven comedies survives, but Athenaeus does provide some reasonably lengthy citations: Cratinus' *Wealth-Gods*, Crates' *Beasts*, Telecleides' *Amphictyons*, Pherecrates' *Miners* and *Persians*, Metagenes' *Thuriopersians* and Nicophon's *Sirens*.

6 In 682 at the mention of the name Hyperbolus Trygaeus exclaims, 'why do you turn your head aside?' This suggests that the statue may have had a movable head, but this may be just a stage direction, enacted only in the minds of those watching.

7 Vienna 1024. See Shapiro (1993: 46, 232), his illustration **9**. He dates the vase 410–400. Shapiro (1993: 46–7, 232), illustration **8** is a sketch of a red-figure *pelike*, 'late fifth century', once in Paris, on which Dionysus and Peace hold the central position, flanked by satyrs and maenads.

8 Pliny the Elder (34.19) dates him to the 102nd Olympiad (372–369).

9 See Lichtenberger et al. (2018, 189–91).

10 Slater (2002: 123).

11 See Lichtenberger et al. (2018: 131–41, 189–91).

12 See Lichtenberger et al. (2018: 157–71). Very little of this complex of buildings survives. It consisted of a forum in front of a temple dedicated to Pax (Peace). Coins minted the reign of Vespasian show Pax holding a cornucopia. The cult statue may have taken this form.

13 As at *Kn.* 1280–9, *Wasps* 1280–3.

14 This has been thoroughly studied by Henderson (1991).

15 On Theoria as a willing sexual participant see Robson (2015) and Sells (2016).

16 Sommerstein (1985: 195) speaks of 'the heavy jocularity associated with weddings both ancient and modern'.

17 For comedy see *Women at the Festival* 163, Callias F 8, Hermippus F 57, Eupolis F 272, Antiphanes F 91; also, Xenophanes F 3, Herodotus 6.12, Thucydides 5.9, 6.77, 7.5, 8.25, Athenaeus 524f.

18 This virtually complete decree directs how Athenian farmers are to send the first-fruits of their produce to the sacred shrine at Eleusis. The allies will be invited, but not commanded, to take part in this offering. Suggested dates range from the 440s to 421. If nearer the latter, it would fit well into a Panhellenic spirit in the late 420s.

19 This latter distinction may have applied to actors and choristers as well.

20 See Sommerstein (1985: 136).

21 'L'attenzione sembra concentrata sul teatro come punto di contatto attori-coro-publico'.

22 The *Tatler*, a weekly journal founded in 1901, described itself as 'an illustrated journal of society and the drama.' Richard King wrote a recurring column called 'Silent Friends'.

23 Jill Paton Walsh, *The Attenbury Emeralds* (London: Hodder, 2010) 101, one of Walsh's continuations of the Lord Peter Wimsey stories by Dorothy L. Sayers.

24 Most think that Cleonymus behaved in a cowardly fashion in battle, perhaps at Delion in late 424, but *Kn.* 1369–72, written months before Delion, suggests that, like the taxiarch at *Peace* 1179–87, he had avoided going out on active service. At 444–6 a would-be taxiarch who opposes peace should 'suffer the same fate as Cleonymus'.

Chapter 5

1 C.S. Lewis, *A Preface to Paradise Lost.* London: Oxford University Press, 1942. Chapter IX.

2 The Athenian Council (*boulē*) was composed of 500 members, fifty from each of the ten tribes. One tribe was in charge for each of the ten months of the calendar year. These were the *prytaneis*.

3 This does not indicate, as some suggest, that the chorus regularly shed their garments in order to dance more freely. The 'gear' is rather the tools mentioned at 299 and 566–7.

4 Principal proponents in the debate include Dale (1957) and Dearden (1976: 20–30) (one door), Dover (1966) and Revermann (2006: 208–9) (more than one door), Sommerstein (1985: xvii) (three).

5 The 2009 production at the University of Newcastle (New South Wales) used one door only and had Hermes depart to the side at 233 and return at 362. At 224–6 Hermes led Trygaeus to the door and pointed in and down to an unseen cave. The rocks were represented by large square stacked blocks that did not block access and were easily moved aside by two chorus-members at 426–30. Ropes were fastened to the statue, not yet visible, and the hauling-scene proceeded.

6 Some ancient sources state that the *ekkyklēma* was a revolving panel in the *skēnē* that displayed the interior scene, but the etymology of 'wheel out' does suggest a raised trolley on wheels.

7 Bellerophon in Euripides' *Stheneboia* and *Bellerophon*, Perseus in his *Andromeda*.

8 Russo 1994 argues that in the late fifth century plays at the Lenaea were performed at a different venue from the Theatre of Dionysus.

9 Pausanias (1.8.2, second century CE) places the statue of Peace and Wealth 'after the statues of the eponymous heroes', that is along the left-hand road of the agora, opposite the public buildings such as the Council Chamber. Isocrates 15.109–10, writing in the 350s, connects the cult of Peace, which 'we celebrate with sacrifices every year', with events in the 370s. He does not provide a location for these sacrifices.

10 Dearden (1976: 13–18) supports the existence of such a platform, Rehm (1988: 306–7) and Olson (1998: xlv) argue against. Marshall (2014: 196–8) suggests that a wooden platform makes the *ekkyklēma* easier to operate, but 'it is certainly mistaken to think of the three actors performing exclusively on a long, thin stage area'.

11 In fifth-century texts *thymelē/thymelikos* refers only to a place for sacrifices with no theatrical association.

12 Rehm (1988: 274) favours a temporary structure that could be adjusted to suit the performance; Marshall (2014: 198–202) prefers a permanent feature. Neither regards the central point as inviolable space. Sommerstein (1985: 178) places the stage-altar in front of the *skēnē*.

13 Rehm (1988: 306).

14 Could the *ekkyklēma* have been wheeled far enough into the *orchēstra* so that the statue could preside from behind the central point where the sacrifice will be attempted?

15 The assignments of the arms-dealer and the sickle-maker could be reversed, but the above scheme has the third actor playing the 'aggressive' roles of War, Hierocles and the arms-dealer.

16 The evidence for comic masks and costumes is well presented by Stone (1984). See also Varakis-Martin (2010) for Aristophanes' use of masks.

17 Documented instances would be Menelaus in *Helen* (412), Telephus in the play of that name (438) and Bellerophon in the tragedy (420s) that inspired *Peace*.

18 *Poetics* 1453a36–8 speaks of a comedy 'where those who are deadliest enemies in the plot, such as Orestes and Aegisthus, exit at the end as new friends, and no one kills anybody'. But we have no hint of what (and when) that comedy could be.

Chapter 6

1 For the second-century CE text of the *Certamen* see West (2003: 297–300, 318–53).

2 The last two lines 1097–8 come directly from Homer *Iliad* 9.63–4.

3 For the *testimonia* to and fragments of *Bellerophon* see Cropp and Collard (2008a: 289–317), also Dobrov (2001) and Dixon (2014). For *Stheneboia* see Cropp and Collard (2008b: 121–41).

4 For *Aeolus* see Collard and Cropp (2008a: 12–31), for *Andromeda* Collard and Cropp (2008a: 124–55), and for *Palamedes* Collard and Cropp (2008b: 46–59).

5 Most of the language here is elevated, but the words *es korakas*, literally 'to the crows', are a colloquial way of saying 'go to blazes' or 'get lost'.

6 These are conveniently set out at Sommerstein (2008: 42–57).

7 The vase is illustrated at Bérard (1974), figure 30. For the fragments of Sophocles' lost satyr-drama see Lloyd-Jones 1996: 250–3.

8 The suggestions by Morosi (2013) that Trygaeus is an 'alter ego' to Prometheus and that the scene in *Peace* with Hierocles the oracle-monger is inspired by Prometheus' claim at 484 to have organized the prophetic arts seem too far-fetched.

9 'Sophocles was a man truly blessed. He lived a long life and died a happy and accomplished man. He came to a fine end, after writing many fine tragedies, never suffering anything bad.'

10 At *Wasps* 1252–5 the elderly Philocleon affirms that 'drinking is a bad thing' but Aristophanes later brings him on very much the worse for wear after a drinking-party. Some have seen this as an allusion to Cratinus' *Wine-Flask* where the elderly poet praises the benefits of drink. See Biles and Olson (2015: xxix–xxxii).

11 See Olson (1998: 216).

12 See the discussion at Biles and Olson (2015: 506).

13 *Peace* would have needed a theatre with a *mēchanē* to be produced properly.

14 *Peace* 73 makes it clear that this beetle comes from Mount Etna, not Attica.

15 Aelian has *agroikos leōs* ('farming folk'), while *Peace* 632 has *ergatēs leōs* ('working folk').

16 On 3 March 2003 The Lysistrata Project arranged for dozens of world-wide readings and productions of the comedy as a protest against a possible American-led invasion of Iraq, which in fact happened two weeks later.

17 The Greek word for Peace was 'Eirene', the source of the English name 'Irene'.

18 This production can be seen at https://www.youtube.com/watch?v=rJs5iOjrNXQ.

19 Flashar (1994: 210), 'Hier wird also erstmals auf der Bühne die politische Dimension der Alten Komödie ernstgenommen, ohne dass der Charakter der Komödie zerstört ware'. Hacks's 1962 East German production and that of Koun in 1977 remain the two most significant modern stagings of *Peace*.

20 From the publicity flyer to be found at http://calliekimball.com/cows-of-war/.

21 'A Hundred Years of the Cambridge Greek Play', a booklet (unpaginated) produced for a 1983 production of Sophocles' *Trachinian Women*, APGRD archive nr. 628.

22 His *Birds* (1959) so offended the political and religious sensibilities of Karamanlis's right-wing régime that further performances were cancelled, causing a storm of protest in the news media. See van Steen (2000: 124–89).

Appendix

1 Plutarch (*Theseus* 24.5) relates an oracle that Athens was like a wine-skin (*askos*) floating on the sea; it might be buffeted, but would never sink.

Glossary

agōn (pl. *agōnes*): 'debate' or 'contest', a formally structured one-on-one exchange between two characters in tragedy and comedy.

anapaest: the metrical unit [∪ ∪ - ∪ ∪ -], the anapaestic tetrameter catalectic was an elevated metre, used in the *agōn* and *parabasis*.

Archidamian War: the first period of the Peloponnesian War, fought between Athens and Sparta, 431–421; ended with the treaty celebrated in *Peace*.

Aristotle: lived 384–322, the famous philosopher resident at Athens, who wrote works in many fields; his *Poetics* is a major source for Athenian tragedy and comedy.

catalectic: a metrical term denoting that the last syllable of the metrical scheme is absent.

chorēgos: a wealthy Athenian who sponsored a dramatic production, providing funds, rehearsal space, maintenance of the chorus etc.

City Dionysia: the major festival at Athens honouring Dionysus, featuring dramatic competitions and lasting for several days in the month of Elaphebolion (late March).

Cleon: a popular demagogue at Athens in the 420s, known for his aggressive style and support for the War, Aristophanes' great foe in his comedies.

Cratinus: career, 454–423, the 'grand old man' of Old Comedy and rival of Aristophanes, his *Wine-Flask* defeated *Clouds* in 423.

dactyl: the metrical unit [- ∪ ∪], the dactylic hexameter was the metre of heroic poetry and oracles.

didascalia: 'production records', lists detailing the production of dramas at Athens, excerpts from which appear in the manuscript tradition.

dimeter: a metrical line that consists of two *metra*.

eisodos: 'way in', one of the two side entrances to the *orchēstra*.

ekkyklēma: 'roll out device', a wheeled platform that was rolled out through the central doors to display an interior scene.

epirrhēma (pl. *epirrhēmata*): a pair of formally corresponding structures found in the *agōn* and *parabasis* of Old Comedy, in an elevated metre.

Eupolis: career, 429–411, successful comic poet closely associated with Aristophanes as both friend and rival; his *Spongers* won first prize at the Dionysia of 421.

exodos: the closing scene of a comedy, usually on a triumphant note, culminating in an exuberant exit procession of actors and chorus.

Hyperbolus: a demagogue, active through the 420s and into the 410s; he 'succeeded' Cleon as the leading popular politician in the Athenian assembly.

hypothesis: an ancient summary of a Greek play, transmitted along with the text, containing a plot and synopsis, and often the details of production.

iamb: the metrical unit [× – ∪ –], where × can be long or short; the iambic trimeter was the principal metre of tragedy and comedy.

kōmōidoumenoi: real persons made fun of in Greek Comedy.

kōmos: a revel or public celebration in the streets; Aristotle claims it as the origin of comic drama.

Lenaea: a festival of Dionysus at Athens, held in the month of Gamelion (late January); from *c.* 440 dramatic competitions were part of this festival.

mēchanē: 'machine', a crane-like device that allowed characters to appear in the air or to make an aerial entrance from behind the *skēnē*-building.

metron: 'measure', the basic unit in Greek metrics; for trochaic, anapaestic, and iambic metres, two feet equal one *metron*; thus 'tetrameter' means four *metra* (eight feet), 'trimeter' three (six feet), and 'dimeter' two (four feet). For dactyls, however, one foot equals one *metron*.

orchēstra: 'dancing-place', a flat area at the foot of the *theatron*, the centre of the playing area.

parabasis (pl. *parabases*): a formally structured part of Old Comedy, usually in the middle of the play, when the actors have left and the chorus address the spectators, both in their own persona and for the poet.

parodos: 'way on', the entry-song of the chorus.

Peace of Nicias: the popular name given to the peace signed between Athens and Sparta in 421.

Pherecrates: career, *c.* 440 to at least 410, an important comic poet who wrote a less 'satirical' and more domestic sort of comedy than Aristophanes.

Platon: career, mid-420s until at least 380, a contemporary and rival comic poet of Aristophanes, he wrote both topical comedy and burlesques of myth.

prologue: the opening scenes of the comedy, in which the characters are introduced and the great idea of the comedy outlined.

satyr-drama: a genre of drama with a chorus of satyrs, which made fun of the traditional myths used in epic and tragedy. In the fifth century a satyr-

drama was written by a tragedian and followed his three tragedies
produced at the City Dionysia.

scholion (pl. scholia, abbreviated as Σ): ancient notes to a classical text,
transmitted along with the text itself in the manuscript tradition. The
author of these notes is called a scholiast.

skēnē: literally 'tent', an architectural structure behind the *orchēstra*, with large
central doors, windows, and a roof (*theologeion*) that could be used as a
playing area.

theatron: both the larger theatrical complex and more narrowly the section
where the spectators (*theatai*) sat and watched.

theologeion: 'place where gods speak', the roof of the *skēnē*-building, which
provided an elevated playing level for dramatic performances.

Thucydides: *c.* 460 – at least 400, Athenian general in the Peloponnesian War
and author of a first-hand historical account of the causes and events of
the conflict.

tetrameter: a metrical line that consists of four *metra*.

trimeter: a metrical line that consists of three *metra*.

trochee: the metrical unit [– ∪ – ×], where × can be long or short; used for
excited entries of the chorus and in the epirrhematic sections of the
parabasis.

Note: Greek metre was not the stressed-based form with which we are
familiar, but a regular pattern of short and long syllables based on time, such
as quarter- or eight-notes in modern music.

Guide to Further Reading and Works Cited

Texts and Commentaries on *Peace*

Henderson 1998: in the familiar format of the Loeb Classical Library, with short introduction, text and facing translation, along with some notes.

Olson 1998: the best modern edition of the comedy, with full introduction and textual history, bibliography, text and extensive commentary.

Platnauer 1964: brief and dated, but the notes in the commentary are still useful.

Sommerstein 1985: the only recent sole-authored English series on Aristophanes' comedies, with short introduction, text and facing translation, and brief notes.

Wilson 2007: the standard edition of the Greek text of Aristophanes.

The scholia to *Peace* have been edited by Holwerda 1982.

Translations

In addition to the above translations by Henderson 1998 and Sommerstein 1985, I would cite Beake 1998, a reasonably accurate translation in free verse; and Sommerstein 1977, a less idiomatic translation than that in Sommerstein 1985, with the spoken scenes in prose and the lyrics in verse.

Monographs on *Peace*

Peace has not been well served by full-length studies of the play. Of the following titles two are collections of individual essays.

Cassio 1985: a collection of thirteen perceptive essays on various aspects of the comedy.

Rochefort-Guillouet, S. 2002: fourteen essays in French, pitched at various levels.

Zogg 2014: a collection and analysis of the various literary allusions in the comedy.

Recommended reading (*) and works cited

*Albini, U. 'La *Pace* di Aristofane, una commedia minore?' *Parola del Passato* 26 (1971): 14–25.

Bastin-Hammou, M. 'Aristophanes' *Peace* on the Twentieth-Century French Stage'. In *Aristophanes in Performance, 421 BC to AD 2007: Peace, Birds, and* Frogs, eds E. Hall and A. Wrigley, 247–54. London: Legenda, 2007.

Beake, F. 'Peace'. In *Aristophanes I*, eds D.R. Slavitt and P. Bovie. Philadelphia: University of Pennsylvania Press, 1998.

Bérard, C. *Anodoi: Essai sur l'imagerie des passages chthoniens*. Rome: Institut Suisse de Rome, 1974.

Biles, Z. and S.D. Olson. *Aristophanes Wasps*. Oxford: Oxford University Press, 2015.

Bowie, A.M. *Aristophanes: Myth, Ritual, and Comedy*. Cambridge: Cambridge University Press, 1993.

*Cassio, A.C. *Commedia e partecipazione: La* Pace *di Aristofane*. Naples: Liguori, 1985.

Collard, C. and M. Cropp. *Euripides Fragments*, 2 vols. Cambridge, MA: Harvard University Press, cited as Collard and Cropp 2008a and 2008b.

Dale, A.M. 'An Interpretation of Ar. *Vesp.* 136–210 and Its Consequences for the Stage of Aristophanes'. *Journal of Hellenic Studies* 77 (1957): 205–11.

de Ste Croix, G.E.M. *The Origins of the Peloponnesian War*. Ithaca: Cornell University Press, 1972.

Dearden, C.W. *The Stage of Aristophanes*. London: Athlone Press, 1976.

Dixon, D. 'Reconsidering Euripides' *Bellerophon*'. *Classical Quarterly* 64 (2014): 493–506.

Dobrov, G.W. 'Bellerophontes: Euripides' *Bellerophontes* and Aristophanes' *Peace*'. In *Figures of Play*, 89–104. Oxford: Oxford University Press, 2001.

Dover, K.J. 'The Skene in Aristophanes'. *Proceedings of the Cambridge Philological Society* 12 (1966): 2–17.

Ferriss-Hill, J.L. *Roman Satire and the Old Comic Tradition*. Cambridge: Cambridge University Press, 2015.

Flashar, H. *Inszenierung der Antike. Das griechische Drama auf der Bühne der Neuzeit 1585–1990*. Munich: Beck, 1991.

Georgosoupolos, K. and S. Gogos *Epidaurus. The Ancient Theatre and Its Performances*. Athens: ISP, 2004.

Given, J. 'Aristophanic Comedy in American Musical Theater, 1925–1969'. In *The Oxford Handbook of Greek Drama in the Americas*, eds K. Bosher et al., 301–32. Oxford: Oxford University Press, 2015.

*Hall, E. 'Casting the Role of Trygaeus in Aristophanes' *Peace*'. In *The Theatrical Cast of Athens*, 321–52. Oxford: Oxford University Press, 2006.

Hall, E. 'Introduction: Aristophanic Laughter across the Centuries'. In *Aristophanes in Performance, 421 BC to AD 2007:* Peace, Birds, *and* Frogs, eds. E. Hall and A. Wrigley, 1–29. London: Legenda, 2007.

Hall, E. and A. Wrigley (eds.). *Aristophanes in Performance, 421 BC to AD 2007:* Peace, Birds, *and* Frogs. London: Legenda, 2007.

Harvey, F.D. 'Sick Humour: Aristophanic Parody of a Euripidean Motif?' *Mnemosyne* 24 (1971): 362–5.

Henderson, J. *The Maculate Muse*, 2nd ed. Oxford: Oxford University Press, 1991.

Henderson, J. *Aristophanes*, vol. II. Cambridge, MA: Harvard University Press, 1998.

Henderson, J. *Aristophanes Fragments*. Cambridge, MA: Harvard University Press, 2007.

Henderson, J. 'Types and Styles of Comedy between 450 and 420'. In *Fragmenta einer Geschichte der griechischen Komödie*, eds. S. Chronopoulos and C. Orth, 146–58. Heidelberg: Verlag Antike, 2015.

Holwerda, D. *Scholia in Aristophanes* (Pars II, Fasciculus II). Groningen, 1982.

*Hubbard, T.K. *The Mask of Comedy: Aristophanes and the Intertextual Parabasis*. Ithaca: Cornell University Press, 1991.

Hughes, A. *Performing Greek Comedy*. Cambridge: Cambridge University Press, 2012.

Kagan, D. *The Archidamian War*. Ithaca NY: Cornell University Press, 1974.

Kiritsi, S. 'Aristophanes, Education, and Performance in Modern Greece'. In *Brill's Companion to the Reception of Aristophanes*, ed. P. Walsh, 67–87. Leiden: Brill, 2016.

Lichtenberger, A., H. Nieswandt and D. Salzmann (eds), *Eirene/Pax: Frieden in der Antike*. Archäologisches Museum der Westfälischen Wilhelms-Universität Münster: Sandstein Verlag, 2018.

Lloyd-Jones, H. *Sophocles Fragments*. Cambridge, MA: Harvard University Press, 1996.

Luppe, W. 'Die Zahl der Konkurrenten an den komischen Agonen zur Zeit des Peloponneischen Krieges'. *Philologus* 116 (1972): 53–75.

MacDowell, D.M. *Aristophanes and Athens*. Oxford: Oxford University Press, 1995.

Marshall, C.W. *The Structure and Performance of Euripides'* Helen. Cambridge: Cambridge University Press, 2014.

Marshall, C.W. and S. van Willigenburg, 'Judging Athenian Dramatic Competitions'. *Journal of Hellenic Studies* 124 (2004): 90–107.

Massey, D. 'Leonard Bernstein and the Harvard Student Union: In Search of Political Origins'. *Journal of the Society for American Music* 3 (2009): 67–84.

Mastromarco, G. 'Dal *Bellerofonte* di Euripide alla *Pace* di Aristofane'. In *Textos fragmentarios del teatro griego antiguo*, eds A. Melero Bellido et al., 93–118. Lecca: Pense Multimedia, 2012.

Mastronarde, D. 'Actors on High: The Skene Roof, the Crane, and the Gods in Attic Drama'. *Classical Antiquity* 9 (1990): 247–94.

*McGlew, J. 'Identity and Ideology: The Farmer Chorus of Aristophanes' *Peace*'. *Syllecta Classica* 12 (2001): 74–97.

*Michelakis, P. 'Mise en scène de *La Paix* d'Aristophane'. In *Analyses et réflexions sur Aristophane: La Paix*, S. Rochefort-Guillouet, 115–17. Paris: ellipses, 2002.

Millis, B.W. and S.D. Olson. *Inscriptional Records for the Dramatic Festivals in Athens*. Leiden: Brill, 2012.

Morosi, F. 'Prometeo Comico: un paradigma trascurato nella *Pace* di Aristofane'. *Dioniso* n.s. 3 (2013): 61–96.

*Moulton, C.H. *Aristophanic Poetry*, Hypomnemata 68. Göttingen: Vandenhoeck & Ruprecht, 1981.

Murray, G. *Aristophanes: A Study*. Oxford: Clarendon Press, 1933.

*Newiger, H.J. 'War and Peace in the Comedy of Aristophanes'. *Yale Classical Studies* 26 (1980): 219–37.

*Olson, S.D. *Aristophanes Peace*. Oxford: Clarendon Press, 1998.

Platnauer, M. *Aristophanes Peace*. Oxford: Clarendon Press, 1964.

Podlecki, A.J. *Perikles and His Circle*. London: Routledge, 1998.

Rehm, R. 'The Staging of Suppliant Plays'. *Greek, Roman and Byzantine Studies* 29 (1988): 263–307.

Revermann, M. *Comic Business. Theatricality, Dramatic Technique, and Performance Contexts of Aristophanic Comedy*. Oxford: Oxford University Press, 2006.

*Robson, J. 'Fantastic Sex: Fantasies of Assault in Aristophanes'. In *Sex in Antiquity*, eds M. Masterson et al., 313–31. London: Routledge, 2015.

Rochefort-Guillouet, S. *Analyses et réflexions sur Aristophane: La Paix*. Paris: ellipses, 2002.

Rosen, R.M. 'The Ionian at Aristophanes *Peace* 46'. *Greek Roman and Byzantine Studies* 25 (1984): 389–96.

Russo, C.F. *Aristophanes: An Author for the Stage*. London: Routledge, 1994.

*Seidensticker, B. 'Aristophanes is Back! Peter Hacks's Adaptation of *Peace*'. In *Aristophanes in Performance, 421 BC to AD 2007*: Peace, Birds, and Frogs, eds E. Hall and A. Wrigley, 194–208. London: Legenda, 2007.

*Sells, D. 'Prostitution and Panhellenism in Aristophanes' *Peace*'. *Archiv für Religionsgeschichte* 17 (2016): 69–90

Shapiro, H.A. *Personifications in Greek Art*. Zurich: Akanthus, 1993.

*Sicking, C.J. 'Aristophanes Laetus?'. In *ΚΩΜΩΙΔΟΤΡΓΑΗΜΑΤΑ• Studia Aristophanea Viri Aristophanei W.J.W. Koster*, ed. R.E.H. Westerdorp Boerma, 115–24. Amsterdam: Hakkert, 1967.

Silk, M. 'Translating/Transposing Aristophanes'. In *Aristophanes in Performance, 421 BC to AD 2007: Peace, Birds, and Frogs*, eds E. Hall and A. Wrigley, 287–308. London: Legenda, 2007.

*Slater, N.W. *Spectator Politics: Metatheatre and Performance in Aristophanes*. Philadelphia: University of Pennsylvania Press, 2002.

Sommerstein A.H. *Aristophanes*. Harmondsworth: Penguin, 1977.

*Sommerstein, A.H. *The Comedies of Aristophanes: Vol. 5, Peace*. Warminster: Aris & Phillips, 1985.

*Sommerstein, A.H. 'Monsters, Ogres and Demons in Old Comedy'. In *Monsters and Monstrosity in Greek and Roman Culture*, ed. C. Atherton, 19–40. Bari: Levante, 1998.

Sommerstein, A.H. *Aeschylus Fragments*, vol. 3. Cambridge MA: Harvard University Press, 2008.

Stafford, E. *Worshipping Virtues: Personification and the Divine in Ancient Greece*. London: Duckworth, 2000.

Steggle, M. 'Aristophanes in Early Modern England'. In *Aristophanes in Performance, 421 BC to AD 2007: Peace, Birds, and Frogs*, eds E. Hall and A. Wrigley, 52–65. London: Legenda, 2007.

Stone, L.M. *Costume in Aristophanic Comedy*. New York: Arno Press, 1981.

Storey, I.C. 'Cutting Comedies'. In *Greek and Roman Drama: Translation and Performance*, ed. J. Barsby, 146–67. Stuttgart: J.B. Metzler, 2002.

*Sulprizio, C. 'You Can't Go Home Again: War, Women, and Domesticity in Aristophanes' *Peace*'. *Ramus* 42 (2013): 44–63.

Taplin. O. *Greek Tragedy in Action*. London: Methuen, 1978.

*Tordoff, R. 'Excrement, Sacrifice, Commensality: The Ophresiology of Aristophanes' *Peace*'. *Arethusa* 44 (2011): 167–98.

van Steen, G. *Venom in Verse: Aristophanes in Modern Greece*. Princeton: Princeton University Press, 2000.

*Vanhaegendoren, K. *Die Darstellung des Friedens in den Acharnern und im Frieden des Aristophanes: stilistiche Untersungen*. Münster: Lit, 1996.

Varakis-Martin, A. 'Body and Mask in Aristophanic Performance'. *Bulletin of the Institute of Classical Studies* 53 (2010): 17–38.

Varakis, A. 'Aristophanic Performance as an All-inclusive Event'. In *Classics in the Modern World: A 'Democratic Turn'?* eds. L. Hardwick and S. Harrison, 213–25. Oxford: Oxford University Press, 2013.

West, M.L. *Homeric Hymns, Homeric Apocrypha, Lives of Homer.* Cambridge, MA: Harvard University Press, 2003.

Whitman, C.H. *Aristophanes and the Comic Hero.* Cambridge, MA: Harvard University Press, 1964.

Wilson, N.G. *Aristophanis Fabulae*, 2 vols. Oxford: Clarendon Press, 2007. Cited as Wilson 2007a and 2007b.

Wright, M. *The Lost Plays of Greek Tragedy*, Volume 2. London: Bloomsbury, 2019.

Yaari, N. 'Constructing Bridges for Peace and Tolerance'. In *Classics in the Modern World: A 'Democratic Turn'?* eds L. Hardwick and S. Harrison, 227–44. Oxford: Oxford University Press, 2013.

Zogg, F. *Lust am Lesen: Literarische Anspielungen im* Frieden *des Aristophanes, Zetemata* 147. Munich: Beck, 2014.

Index